RECIPE *for*
RECOVERY

RECIPE *for* RECOVERY

A Guide to the Twelve Steps of Chronic Pain Anonymous

Chronic Pain Anonymous Service Board

ISBN: 978-0-9856524-5-6

Library of Congress Control Number: 2015935753

Chronic Pain Anonymous Service Board
8924 East Pinnacle Peak Road
Suite G5-628
Scottsdale, AZ 85255
Website: *http://www.chronicpainanonymous.org*

CPA Conference Approved

First Edition

#301

The meaning of these Steps is based in faith, humility, and the ability to turn over the problems of our life to a greater power, without trying to control or direct the outcome.

—Dale L., Cofounder of Chronic Pain Anonymous

CPA Serenity Prayer

God, grant me the serenity
to accept the things I cannot change,
the courage to change the things I can,
and the wisdom to know the difference.
Thy will, not mine, be done.

Contents

Foreword

Sitting in my home in Maryland in late 2001, I started to experience pain in my chest and back. Initially it was a mild, intermittent sensation that was located in a band around my body where I recently had surgery to remove a tumor from inside my spinal cord.

One of the lasting aftereffects of my surgery was that I had lost all sensation from the nipple line of my chest to my toes. The pain I was feeling was in the boundary area between where I had sensation and where I had none. At first I ignored the issue, but over several weeks, the pain increased in severity, duration, and frequency. I called the surgeon for an appointment to find out what was causing my pain.

When I sat down with the doctor, he was not surprised by my situation. He told me that often when people have surgery to their spinal cord or have a spinal cord injury, one of the issues they may experience is neuropathic pain. Neuropathic pain, also known as nerve pain, is a type of chronic pain that can occur when the nerves have been damaged or injured. The doctor apologized for not informing me of this potential side effect of the surgery.

The question was, what do I do now? There were few options. I could try narcotics to dull the pain, and there were other medications I could try to lessen the effects. He said we would just have to experiment and see what would work best for me.

As a recovering alcoholic who lived thirty years self-medicating my physical and emotional pain, narcotics were out of the question. I knew firsthand what it was like to dull my mind with alcohol and drugs. I'd lived that life and didn't wish to return. I asked if there were any other medications I could use. We settled on a strong pain medication recommended as a first-line agent to treat neuropathic pain. I started at the minimum dosage, twice a day.

As time passed, into the summer and fall of 2002, I found my pain increasing, as well as my dosage of the drug. In late fall, I was at the maximum dosage a person can safely take daily. My pain was still present, the severity and duration were increasing, and the side effects of the medication were beginning to have an effect on my mental and emotional functions. I have always been an avid reader, but I was finding my ability to concentrate was very limited. I was starting to withdraw from my family and friends. I was finding any reason possible to avoid activities that included interaction with other people. I was lying and making excuses for my behavior. I was short-tempered with my wife and young son. I had become an irritable and disagreeable person. Doctors were supplementing my dosage with other medications that had their own side effects, all of which were making me even more unpleasant to be around. Deep inside, I knew there had to be a better way.

One day in early 2003, I was talking with my Alcoholics Anonymous (AA) sponsor about what was going on in my life. A few days earlier, my wife had commented that I was acting much like I did when I was drinking and she didn't like seeing those days returning. I explained this to my sponsor, and we both came to the realization that I could try the Twelve Steps of AA as a tool to work with pain. After all, people were using the Twelve Steps for eating disorders, narcotics, gambling, and a host of other obsessions. So I set out to adapt the Steps, focusing on chronic pain.

Step One: "We admitted we were powerless over *pain*—that our lives had become unmanageable." That was absolutely the case with me. I was totally powerless over my pain. I had tried for many months to manipulate my pain, to eradicate my pain, to alter my pain. I tried drugs, yoga, acupuncture, everything I could think of or had heard about, but I was still in pain and at its mercy. It was easy for me to accept that whatever I tried didn't work and that my pain won out. I was totally powerless.

My life was a shambles. I was at odds with my wife, my son, and the world at large. Everything about my life was starting to unravel. Was my life unmanageable? Undeniably, yes.

I immersed myself in Step One for a few weeks to let it set in. Over the course of this short time, I realized that my relationship with my pain was changing. It was no longer adversarial.

I went on to Step Two: "Came to believe that a Power greater than ourselves could restore us to sanity." That was easy for me. After working the Steps in AA, I had a Higher Power that had relieved me from alcohol and drug abuse. I knew this could happen again.

So I moved on to Step Three: "Made a decision to turn our will and our lives over to the care of God, as we understood Him." I did this one easily, and the tension in my life soon diminished.

As I was working through the Steps as applied to pain, I realized my life and attitude were improving. Was my pain lessening? I didn't believe so, but the stranglehold it had on my life was diminishing. Once I got to Step Eleven—"Sought through prayer and meditation to improve our conscious contact with God *as we understood Him,* praying only for knowledge of His will for us and the power to carry that out"—my life and my state of mind began to shift. When I started utilizing meditation to get through the truly tough pain moments or days, I found I was becoming myself again.

Now I needed to practice Step Twelve and give my recovery away to others. In June 2004, I was speaking at an AA meeting in Baltimore. I spoke about how I was using the Steps of AA for living with my chronic pain. I spoke of the serenity and peace I was experiencing from staying true to the Twelve-Step path with another obsession. After the meeting, a man spoke with me about how he, too, was using the Twelve Steps to deal with his pain. We went to have coffee, which resulted in the two of us holding our first Chronic Pain Anonymous (CPA) meeting, right there and then.

We located a church to schedule weekly meetings. We contacted AA to get approval to use the Twelve Steps and other AA material. We set up a website to attract other people, and that is how we began this journey. Over the course of a few years, we found many in our CPA fellowship didn't have pain as their primary issue but lived with chronic illness. To accommodate their inclusion, we added the words "chronic illness" to our Steps and all our literature.

What follows in this book are the Steps we take in recovery from the obsessive desire to control our chronic pain and chronic illness and the harmful effects it has had on our lives. We are sharing the tools we used to realize this recovery.

Many who join our fellowship have no experience in other Twelve-Step programs and don't know how to work the Steps. Others are familiar with the Twelve Steps and have not yet applied them to pain and illness. This book is a step-by-step guide to support us in our recovery and as a resource when we sponsor each other on this journey. It was created to make the Steps available to everyone who lives with chronic pain and illness, so that they can realize there is an abundance of life available to us all, in spite of our afflictions.

These Steps have helped me to live a life where I can once again contribute to myself, my family, and others. I pray they can do the same for you.

In Service,

Dale L., CPA Cofounder
St. Thomas, Virgin Islands, 2015

The Doctor's Opinion

My belief in the importance and deep need for Chronic Pain Anonymous (CPA) is based on both the prevalence of chronic pain and illness I see as a neurosurgeon and my personal experience working and living the Twelve Steps. I have practiced for thirty-six years as a board-certified neurosurgeon and am also certified by the American Board of Pain Medicine to practice pain medicine, which is of increasing demand as the problems of chronic pain and chronic illness escalate.

More than 100 million people in the United States alone have chronic pain. Half of all adults have a chronic illness. Adding to the problem are aging baby boomers and advances in medicine that prolong life. The cost to care for these people is increasing exponentially, ransacking Medicare and Social Security. Yet chronic pain and illness are much more than statistics; people who struggle with chronic pain and illness experience physical, emotional, and spiritual agony.

In my work, I have treated thousands of patients with chronic pain and illness. The spectrum of diagnoses is vast: traumatic brain injury; stroke; brain tumor; spinal injury, with varying degrees of paralysis; back and extremity pain from degenerated spine disease; Parkinson's disease; multiple sclerosis; seizures; and multiple other conditions.

Many of my patients are acutely ill, and while I have watched some die as I fought to save their lives, most of my patients, thankfully, survive in good health. Still, others live battling chronic pain and chronic illness. These individuals exist in fear, depression, victimization, anger, denial, addiction, guilt, resentment, and isolation. Desperate for relief, they endure one failed procedure after another until finally there are no more procedures available. What's left? Medication. Those with chronic pain and illness often jump from pill to pill—dazed from multiple medications, plagued by the medications' side effects—sometimes developing a tolerance and thus taking more pills than prescribed.

So it's no surprise that drug-related death due to misuse and abuse of prescriptions is also a growing problem. Obviously, not every patient who misuses or abuses medication dies. However, for each patient who dies, there are numerous others who suffer less final consequences: on average, 32 more will require emergency room visits and another 130 will seek outpatient clinic services because of misuse and abuse of prescriptions. And not all drugs used by chronic-pain sufferers are prescribed or even legal. People self-medicate using marijuana, alcohol, "street" drugs, or a combination of these, both legally and illegally, often to addictive effect.

The medical world isn't blind to the problem. In 1995, the American Pain Society declared that a patient's pain should be of greater concern and more aggressively treated than it had been in the past. Now pain is the fifth vital sign—along with pulse, temperature, respiration, and blood pressure—used to assess a patient. The first four vital signs are objective, clearly read with the right instruments. Pain assessment, on the other hand, is subjective and dependent on how the patient describes it. So pain level can be overstated or understated, making it more elusive to treat than, say, high blood pressure or poor respiration. Many physicians play a guessing game, trying to help a patient's pain with various medications. The number of prescriptions written and filled has quadrupled in the recent past, in part because of Medicare policies and the increased manufacturing of new narcotics and anxiety and sleep medications.

The Institute of Medicine has recommended a social transformation in the way pain and illness are perceived, judged, and treated. I agree. Physicians and individuals with chronic illness and chronic pain need to know and accept the limits of medicine. Writing and filling prescriptions is not the complete answer. People, both within and outside the medical field, need to listen to these suffering individuals with compassion and understanding and offer hope and support. This is where CPA plays a major role.

I see so many patients with chronic pain and illness—people who have lost faith, are helpless, and seek peace in vain. I realized the Twelve Steps could help them and sought to put my patients in touch with a program that changed my life. I discovered CPA, specifically for those with chronic pain and illness. With help from CPA, I organized a local group, through which I work to bring hope to those who feel hopeless.

I have worked the Twelve Steps for the last sixteen years, and I continue my recovery in the program, for which I am so grateful. In working the Twelve Steps, I am empowered to be vulnerable and to share my deepest fears and darkest secrets with my Higher Power and my sponsor, both of whom extend unconditional love to me. My sponsor was the first of many friends I have made through the Twelve Steps. In this fellowship, I discovered a spiritual awakening, which has bolstered my trust in and reliance on my Higher Power. To this Higher Power I have surrendered and found a new freedom and happiness. It's not only me. In the program, I regularly witness individuals who, having accepted their helplessness to fix their problems, find strength, solutions, and spiritual awakening. It is about holding on to hope and eventually finding peace.

Maybe it helps to think of it like this: Imagine the Twelve Steps as a large room with many doors through which you may enter (like CPA or Alcoholics Anonymous). Outside of these doors, you feel alone or defeated or too broken to be fixed. Maybe you feel all those things. Maybe even right now you're stuck. The way out is by going in. Stepping into the Twelve-Step room. It doesn't matter what door you walk through; once inside, you see we are all broken. We all feel alone. We are all defeated. We are, in fact, much the same, and we all need each other, along with our Higher Power, to restore one another, to save one another from fear and self-centeredness, to walk with one another, even when the path is a daunting one.

I invite you today, at this very moment, to find your door into the Twelve-Step room, a door into hopefulness. I invite you to accept the serenity to live one day at a time, enjoying one moment at a time, accepting hardships as a passageway to peace, and trusting that as you surrender to your Higher Power, you will find strength and an unfathomable peace.

Dr. Ron
Tulsa, OK
2015

Preface

Many of us with chronic pain and chronic illness have cognitive and energy deficits, and reading can be challenging and overwhelming. We have written this book to present the Twelve Steps in a way that is manageable for anyone, whatever their condition.

Just like a recipe in a cookbook, we have put the Chronic Pain Anonymous (CPA) Twelve Steps into simple and accessible terms so anyone who so desires can use this effective tool of recovery. These Steps are a logical process by which we find recovery, defined as the ability to live peacefully, joyfully, and comfortably with ourselves and others.

This book will acquaint the newcomer as well as current members with the CPA way of life. It is literature to help us all be successful in recovery. It is written in the voices of the longtime members of the fellowship, passing on their experience, strength, and hope. May you find what you need here, right now.

About Step Study

Chronic Pain Anonymous (CPA) is not a religion or a therapy program. We are a fellowship of friends who live with chronic pain and chronic illness. We pass along the CPA program as practiced by the early members. This is a "we" program. We study and discuss the Steps together, and we recover together. We share a simple program of twelve suggested Steps that can be completed over a short period of time.

The Steps are the heart of the CPA program of recovery. They are not just talked about but are acted upon so they can result in a spiritual awakening. Faith alone is not sufficient. We are required to take the necessary actions in order to have a transformation of attitude and behavior. Although they are studied with a sponsor, applying the principles of each Step is done individually. Understanding and putting these Steps into practice is life-changing. Doing this can alleviate the negative effects of living with chronic pain and chronic illness.

When we arrive at CPA, we generally have lost all hope for serenity or happiness. We are told there is a way to regain these, to enjoy life no matter what is happening with our physical condition. We hear a message of hope, that there is a common solution, a way out of our misery and suffering. Until now, life seemed impossible, and our situation was intolerable. We were desperate, having tried everything to find relief and/or a cure. We discovered no lasting solutions for our health challenges. In CPA, we learn that only a spiritual solution will transform our lives and bring us peace.

In order to do this, we must undergo a deep transformation. We may not want to hear this. We want the magic elixir that will cure us and make our pain and illness disappear. What is offered in CPA is a revolutionary concept. It offers a solution that is based not on medicinal fixes but on walking a spiritual path of recovery that has worked for a multitude of people worldwide. Without it, we may find we continue to live depressed, angry, and isolated lives.

The good news is, a spiritual experience is not only possible; it can become our reality—if we keep an open mind and take the Steps as described in this book. There is hope for everyone, regardless of what has happened in the past. Whether we've lived in denial or spent many dollars searching for cures, whether we have strong religious beliefs or none, it doesn't matter. We can start this program without any spiritual beliefs. All we need is willingness, honesty, and an open mind. It is enough to believe that *others* believe the program works and to believe that the Twelve Steps have raised the quality of life for countless people.

"Higher Power" (HP, for short) is simply a Power greater than ourselves. There is a long list of names people use when referring to this, such as God, Universal Mind, Holy Spirit, Jesus, Divine Mother, Buddha, Allah. These words are often related to specific religious traditions. Such traditions are not part of CPA, and members are free to refer to the Power greater than oneself by any name they are comfortable with and with any understanding that brings them closer to it. Whether we arrive here as a member of a religious organization or as an atheist or agnostic, we will reap the benefits of working the Twelve Steps.

This may be a revolutionary way of thinking for some or quite familiar. We have found that no matter what we believe or call it, this Power is accessible to each of us.

When we follow these simple Steps and work them with honesty and due diligence, we will experience something miraculous and begin recovering from the destructive effects of chronic pain and illness. Changing our thinking will lead to changing our actions. We will begin to live in the *now*, letting go of the "yesterdays and tomorrows." We will take the necessary actions to move forward in our lives successfully, guided by our Higher Power. In this way, we will be led to a new sense of joy and serenity.

The Steps are suggestions. There are no rules or regulations. The decision to work these Steps is ours to make.

HOW DO WE DO IT?

First we need to understand each Step, and we usually learn about them by "working" them with the help of our sponsor—a fellow member we meet in CPA whom we trust and who has worked the Steps before us. We attend meetings, talk to our friends in the fellowship, and read CPA literature. We learn how each Step relates to our lives. Then we make a conscious effort to change our behavior and thinking according to the principles of the Step. *How does it apply to my situation, and how can I integrate what I am learning into my life?* This is what it means to "work" the Steps. It takes time to change a lifetime of habits, and so this is a moment-by-moment program. There is no rush.

We want to be thorough, and timing is different for each of us. However, the sooner we work the Steps, the sooner we can experience the benefits of recovery. There is no single approach, but it is best to take them one at a time, in order, just as we do to follow a recipe. Each Step builds on those that come before it.

Working the Steps is a process that makes it possible to awaken new awareness, strength, and hope. It leads to a celebration of life. The Twelve Steps allow us to become more than we ever imagined. We no longer have to struggle, alone and lost. The Steps show us the way to come alive in ways we have not known previously or have forgotten long ago. They help us welcome love and joy into our lives. We become open to the grace that is available to all of us.

A NOTE ON HOW THE BOOK IS ORGANIZED

Each chapter will have a list of "Ingredients," the psychological, emotional, and spiritual aspects that best go into working that Step; a "Description" of what the Step will help us learn and discover and lead us to on this journey; and "Directions," which are ways that members have worked on the Step. Feel free to use these Directions exactly as suggested or as jumping-off points and inspiration for you and your sponsor. At the end of each Directions section, you'll find "Working the Step," a list of questions to help you delve deeper and explore all facets of that Step. The "What It Looks Like" section ends each chapter. These are personal experiences, written by the men and women of CPA, who describe how they applied a Step when living with chronic pain and chronic illness. They illustrate what the Step looks like when it is applied in one's daily life.

The book concludes with stories of CPA recovery, written by members of the fellowship who share what their lives were like before working the Steps, how they practiced the Steps, and what their lives look like today.

For simplicity's sake, we have chosen to use "God" and "Higher Power" when referring to a Power greater than ourselves, as these terms are familiar to most of us. However, we invite each reader to insert his or her personal attribution for this Source that is greater than us and to not let a name become a distraction. This also applies to the use of "He" when a pronoun is needed, as it does not imply that our Higher Power has a specific gender or any gender. It is merely a common convention and keeps it simple. (In the stories at the end of the book, members will refer to their Higher Power in their own way, as "He," "She," or with no attribution.)

There are as many ways to work the Steps as there are members of the fellowship. May the ones suggested here guide you on your personal path to recovery from the effects of chronic pain and chronic illness.

Step One

We admitted we were powerless over chronic pain and chronic illness—that our lives had become unmanageable.

Ingredients

Surrender
Acceptance of powerlessness
Acceptance of the unacceptable
Teachability
Willingness

Description

Step One identifies the problem. The rest of the Steps focus on the solution. In this Step, we drop any pretense and become honest with ourselves. We admit that we have been holding on to both an illusion of and a strong desire for power over our pain and illness. We willingly look at the ways in which our lives have become unwieldy and impossible to manage, how this causes us pain above and beyond the physical, and we are not afraid to name them. From this place of admission and acceptance, we can relax, perhaps for the first time in a long time, and look forward to the real possibility of recovery.

Directions

What is our problem? It is our obsession with our physical condition and the desire to make the pain and illness go away. We dwell on our health problems constantly and are fixated on finding answers and relief. This obsession keeps us up at night and makes our days a living agony. It is this craving, this desire for things to be different that makes our lives so unhappy. We blame our despair, loneliness, anger, and fear on our chronic pain and illness. The state of our physical being has become our master and seems to control our happiness.

We try many different ways to fight the pain and illness. We talk about it incessantly, see multiple health-care providers, read everything we can about our condition. Nothing works, and rather than accept our powerlessness, we sink lower and lower in our misery.

In Step One, we become aware of all the ways our lives are unmanageable and how we have gotten lost and confused. Our physical illness and pain have led to mental and emotional pain. We recognize that our obsession over it has had devastating consequences in our lives. The CPA solution is to surrender and admit, fully, that we cannot control our pain and illness. We concede that we are, indeed, powerless over it.

Surrender is the essential ingredient. After years of trying to fix our condition, being at war with it, trying to control it, we finally accept we can't alter the situation. Just doing this is a remarkable accomplishment. This is the first part of the First Step in recovery—admitting we are powerless.

It may seem counterintuitive, but in fact it works. As long as we deny our powerlessness, our problem cannot be solved. Admitting powerlessness opens the door to the solution. Surrender leads to acceptance of the unmanageability of our lives. We see more clearly what is not working. When we accept our powerlessness, we become teachable and willing.

To bring about this acceptance, it helps to identify specific examples of ways in which our lives are unmanageable and we are powerless. This helps us begin to see through new eyes. For example, perhaps we have stopped attending family functions that we used to look forward to with all our hearts, or we may decline invitations from friends because we don't know if we will have the energy when the day arrives. We become aware that we are isolating ourselves and are missing out on sharing in life's joys.

If we find we are struggling to begin, we can pray for the willingness to work this First Step. We need to be able to feel our powerlessness over pain and illness and connect with the emotional despair and suffering that result when our lives are unmanageable. Surrender means to accept things as they are, not trying to change anything. This does not mean we stop medications or the current treatment or palliative activities our health-care providers have recommended. We simply accept that what we have been doing has not been the solution we were seeking. Though this may be painful, *it is the way out*—by going through what we have been avoiding.

It is an irony of the Steps that through acceptance of what we can and can't control, by accepting the unacceptable, we find freedom *and* our personal power. We are powerless but not helpless. No matter where we go, our body goes with us. We can't escape or run away from the symptoms and sensations. And we can't control them. So it is time to accept the situation as it is and let go of trying to change it.

We did not cause, we cannot control, and we cannot cure our chronic pain and illness. All our attempts to push against our situation and control it have led to our lives becoming unmanageable. When we stop seeing our bodies and conditions as the enemy and adjust our attitude toward compassion and acceptance, a new, satisfying, abundant life is possible. We learn that we are powerless but certainly not hopeless.

This may seem confusing at first. We are terrified to just *let go* and *let things be* for this moment. We are used to feeling like we have to be on high alert and vigilant all the time. But this attitude has damaged our relationships with others and made us miserable in our own bodies.

It isn't until we let go of the illusion that we are in control, always chasing after the magical cure—the "answer" to our health problems, the surefire solution—that we can begin to move toward a productive and healthy direction in our lives. It is when we let go completely that we begin to find solutions *not of our doing*.

To find peace, serenity, and joy in our lives, we are going to have to change—to do things differently. We need to have an honest relationship with our pain and illness, to admit we are powerless over them. When we do, they will no longer define our lives.

When we get this honest with ourselves, when we surrender and accept, when we become willing and teachable, what next becomes clear is this: We can't make this change alone. We must ask for help. That is when we move on to Step Two, where we learn that help is ready and available.

Working the Step

1. Have I made a list of specific ways I am powerless over pain and illness?

2. What does "admitting powerlessness" mean to me?

3. How important is control to me?

4. In what ways do I recognize that my life is unmanageable?

5. What keeps me holding on to the illusion that I can control chronic pain and illness?

6. What does "surrender" mean to me? What ways do I struggle with the surrender suggested in this Step?

7. What does being teachable mean to me? How does it manifest in my life?

8. What does willingness feel like to me? How do I recognize when I am willing?

9. How would my life look if I were relieved of the emotional pain that is part of my condition and circumstances?

What It Looks Like

I came to CPA because I felt like I was going crazy on the inside. The First Step made me look at some of the things I was trying to hang on to, such as what I thought I ought to still be able to do (which included all the things I was able to before, despite the fact that I was in pain). This state of mind caused me more pain—and then it just created more unmanageability. As I wrote out my First Step, I began to see the things I was trying to accomplish. Even as I would think about them, I'd think about the pain they were causing me. It allowed me to begin to admit that my body is not the same as it was before I had chronic pain and illness. There were so many things I kept trying to do, and I kept trying to pretend that nothing had changed in my life. I think by writing out the things that seemed to cause me more pain, the things that seemed completely out of control, I was able to find the common denominator: *my body is not the same.*

Until I was really able to write that all down, I don't think I was willing to admit it. And my inability to admit that my body wasn't the same was causing huge emotional turmoil. Everything was incredibly emotional, even simple tasks—just fixing dinner became a huge emotional encounter for me and my mom, who lives with me. Going to work was an emotional encounter for everyone I worked with. I was really grateful to be able to sit down and write it down. I don't think I have to like that I have chronic pain and chronic illness, but I do have to admit it. And then from there I can make a choice: Do I want to keep fighting it, or do I want to learn how to work as harmoniously with it as I can?

~

I set to work on Step One after some hemming and hawing on whether I really needed to be here or not. It wasn't until I did a complete, written First Step inventory of how every aspect of my life has been affected as a person with chronic pain. Slowly, I was able to let go of "acting as if I was healthy and normal" and let go of the fantasy of returning to "my old normal." I set out to discover what "my new normal" is, one day at a time. I cried and grieved as I let go of my trusty, reliable athletic body and slowly began to learn and accept that every area of my life had become unmanageable. My ego did not want to believe and accept this "new normal." I grieved, and slowly, as I felt the feelings and moved through the feelings, I began to understand and accept my situation. With the patience and love of folks in CPA, I began to learn a new vocabulary in caring for myself and began to practice acceptance at a level I never knew before.

~

When I think of what "unmanageable" means to me, I think of frustration and confusion and stress. The more I try to control my life and keep on going despite pain and illness, the worse I feel physically, which makes it even more difficult to keep up with everything, which makes me more depressed and anguished and angry. It is a never-ending cycle of working and striving, resulting in increased pain, then getting upset and hurting even more physically but not knowing what else to do or how else to function. One of the wonderful things about this program is learning to accept that I am powerless and my life is unmanageable. It is like taking a deep breath and feeling the relief of surrender.

~

We admitted we were powerless over pain and illness. This can sound like a really bad idea. Admit I am powerless? It is easy to see how this can seem to indicate weakness, being spineless, giving up, and self-pity. I have learned, however, that admitting I am powerless over this condition is liberating.

Yes, I have some control, some of the time, over how I feel. If I choose to go jogging or move some heavy boxes, my pain will increase immensely for days or probably weeks. If I choose to go for a twenty-minute walk every day, I will probably feel better. If I choose to stay up late, for whatever reason, I won't get enough sleep and my pain the next day will be greatly increased. If I choose instead to get the needed sleep, my pain usually will be less. What I eat or don't eat can make a difference. There are many things I can do to control, to a certain degree, how I feel some of the time, but the fact is that I am powerless over the fact that I have this condition.

~

My experience when I began Step One in CPA was that I first needed to let go totally of thinking about ways to end the pain and symptoms of illness. I had to admit and accept that I was powerless. Period. This was liberating. I had spent mega time, money, and energy seeking solutions to problems that did not have clear-cut answers. I was broke, hopeless, and worn down from the war I had been waging. Being given permission to let go and admit I had no power, no control over my pain and illness, was a gift. It gave a much-needed easing of the stress of battling with my body, the doctors, and the health-care system.

Step One made it possible to just live. Just be. I could enjoy the birds singing in the trees outside the kitchen window. I could enjoy the blessings in my life, such as my home, my friends, and the abilities that were intact. I had forgotten what it was like to enjoy life, to merely be alive and not try to fix every pain and every symptom. Step One opened the door to end the fighting. In the admission of powerlessness, I could surrender into the peace of the present moment. My recovery journey began from the stillness of surrender.

~

In terms of my life being unmanageable, all I can say right now is that every relationship in my life went through enormous changes as a result of my illness and pain but mostly as a result of how I tried to manage the symptoms. I had much to learn about letting go of my assumptions about who I am and who other people are and *how* or *whether* they belong in my life. For me, pain and illness involve loss and having to let go. What I have come to learn are the ways my life had become unmanageable and that some things are worth losing. Once upon a time, I hated change. Now I expect it. I don't always welcome it, but I do know it will happen; it is happening all the time. Trying to hold on has caused me some of the greatest pain in my life, and learning how to let go has helped me more than I can say.

~

The first thing I want to say about Step One is that I've never done it perfectly. I've never done it for the last time. I wished I had known that when I first started working the Steps. With the First Step, I realized I was powerless and my life was unraveling and spinning out of control because of my reaction to pain and illness; it had gone on for decades. It was a relief to finally see that my life was unmanageable and I am powerless.

~

As I worked Step One in CPA, recently, I found the complexities of admitting powerlessness were different with chronic illness and pain than in my other Twelve-Step work. This was confusing and caused angst. On the one hand, trying to control and fix things has caused a lot of the distress and emotional pain, but on the other hand, I do think it's important to be open to how we can help ourselves. After reading, writing, and talking with my sponsor, it came to me very clearly and succinctly: I am not responsible for creating or causing these medical conditions that bring me pain. That was the clarity I needed to really work Step One.

I think perhaps the clarity may be different for each of us. For me, I was relieved of the illusion of "power" to imagine that I could fix, deny, or cure. And as I work to understand the unmanageability, I see that I create it most dramatically when I forget that I didn't create this condition or bring it about. And when I forget this, I end up angry at myself because I haven't fixed it, taken better care, and so on. When I remember—and I'm working on this—that I didn't cause it, I can be kinder to myself, and it's so much easier to take care with kindness when I haven't entered into a war zone with myself.

~

I struggled with understanding the acceptance part of our pain and illness without giving up hope or doing anything about getting healthy. It took me awhile to figure out what this meant for me and the balance it involves. Something came out of my mouth today when someone asked me about it. They said they didn't know how to give up hope on getting better. I said, "I changed what I hope for. Instead of hoping for a cure, I hope that I will be happy just the way I am." Yes, I still have that hope for a cure, way back in my head, but it isn't my dominant thought anymore. Because I found CPA, I have learned to accept what I have and try to find ways to be happy today in the middle of it all.

Step Two

Came to believe that a Power greater than ourselves could restore us to sanity.

Ingredients

Willingness to believe there is a Power greater than ourselves

Simplicity

Accepting life on life's terms

Understanding that our Higher Power can restore us

Description

This phrase has often been heard at Twelve-Step meetings: *"We came, we came to, we came to believe."*

In Step One, we showed up at meetings ("came") and woke up to the fact that we are powerless and cannot face our recovery from chronic pain and illness alone ("came to"), and in Step Two, we "come to believe." This Step brings us real hope. We have surrendered our attachment to controlling the situation, and now we can be open to the solution, which is beyond the limitations of our current understanding.

Directions

How do we find the Power that is greater than ourselves? Most often, the way to do this is to remove what is in our way of recognizing it. The Power is already there and always has been—we just have been unable to see it.

Often, arrogance and self-will are what block us from seeing the spiritual solution. We may have old concepts of a Higher Power that have not served us, so it takes a willingness to let go of our preconceived notions and consider a new concept. Or, right now, we may not be able to conceive of such a Power at all. All we have to do in Step Two is be willing to accept it as a possibility. Where do we find this willingness? Illness and pain have pushed us to our edge. From the depths of our ongoing suffering and hopelessness we find motivation for our *willingness to believe.*

What can be hard to understand about the first part of this Step is its simplicity. We seek more complex answers. But truly, *all* we need to do is be willing to believe in a Power greater than ourselves. This is an essential ingredient in our program of recovery.

This Power is one of our own understanding. No one defines it for us. If we are willing to seek our own concept, we will find one that works for us.

There are as many different versions of a Higher Power as there are people in recovery. Some people see nature in all its wonder and beauty as a Power greater than themselves. They can understand and are willing to believe in nature. Others, who do not warm to the concept of a "God" at all, may use the fellowship as their Higher Power. Still others, who perhaps have been raised in a religious tradition and practice it, will use their familiar concept of a Higher Power. There are those who wish to completely create their Higher Power with their own imagination, giving it the most loving attributes they can conceive of. These are just a few possible ways to become willing to believe.

The concept of this Higher Power doesn't matter; it doesn't have to look any particular way. This Step just requires that we have one. We need to accept there is a Higher Power and we are not it, even if we may feel it as within us. This Power supports our well-being and has an energy of unconditional love. It is this Power, and this Power alone, that can restore us to sanity.

Insanity has been described as doing the same thing over and over, expecting different results. We each have our own version of insanity, ways in which we do not live in reality. Ways in which we do not accept life on life's terms. Perhaps we continue to view ourselves as essentially healthy, saying so to doctors and friends, attempting the same activities and chores as we did before pain or illness, resulting in greater frustration and even more pain or increased symptoms. Or we may go from doctor to doctor, seeking the medication or operation to cure us. We may overdo it physically, knowing we should have stopped sooner, but we kept going, hoping this time would be different.

Our Higher Power can restore us to sanity—to soundness of mind, heart, and spirit. We have to do the work. Our work is the Steps. We have already begun by working Step One.

When we simply accept that our own capabilities have not been able to change reality and we seek help from a higher source, sanity becomes possible. We give up the insanity of trying to control the uncontrollable. We come to understand that only a Power greater than ourselves can restore us, because clearly, our own thinking has not been effective in doing so. We surrender, are willing to believe, and find ourselves restored.

How do we come to this understanding? We discover in meetings and fellowship that others are not as confused or anxious as we are, that there is a sense of peace in meetings. Other people seem to be happy, even though they are also physically ill and/or in pain. We consider that we may be able to believe in a Power greater than ourselves who can help us, too. We don't have to believe that a Power greater than us will restore us to sanity, we only have to believe that it may happen, that it could happen.

Some of us who do not believe that a Higher Power exists may come to this Step and, because we are either atheist or agnostic, stop and go no further. There is reason to continue. There is hope. We have among us people who questioned this Step and were easily able to move forward by finding something else outside of themselves to serve as a Higher Power. As mentioned earlier, some have designated the fellowship or even their home group as a Power greater than themselves. Some find their Higher Power in nature or the arts. Some people use their sponsor's belief until they come to one on their own.

Those of us who already have a strong relationship with our Higher Power learn to let that Higher Power have access to this area of our lives and become willing to let our Higher Power restore us to sanity.

We do not concern ourselves with what others believe in this area—we take what we like, leave the rest, and let others do the same, so that all can have the opportunity to benefit from the wealth of this program.

Our Higher Power is loving, caring, and will provide for us. If, at first, we have doubts about this, or about its existence, our group and our sponsor may be our strongest links to our "HP."

We have choices. If coming to believe feels really difficult, a great way to work this Step is to act "as if" we have faith. Using the Serenity Prayer will also help with this Step. (The Serenity Prayer is found in the front pages of this book.)

We will use this Step again and again. Whenever we lose hope—when we feel lost and confused, scared and lonely—we can come back to Step Two and find a source of help, comfort, and guidance that is beyond our own limitations and abilities. We discover that it is always there. One day at a time, we come to believe that help is always available, regardless of our circumstances.

In this Step, we are allowing the possibility that there could be a Power that exists in our lives, beyond our ego, beyond self-generated solutions. It is a huge relief.

Working the Step

1. Have I prayed for the willingness to be willing to work this Step?

2. How do my previous experiences with religion and spirituality affect what I believe today about a Power greater than myself? What works for me? What needs to be reassessed?

3. Can I conceive of a Power great enough to restore me to sanity, even if, just for today, I may not believe it will do so?

4. How do I know there is a Higher Power and that I am not it?

5. Do I sense spiritual guidance in my life? How?

6. What is my concept of a Higher Power today? What attributes do I give my Higher Power?

7. What, if anything, keeps me from accepting a Higher Power? What is needed to move toward acceptance?

8. What does "sanity" mean to me? What does it look like in my life?

9. What behaviors do I keep doing while expecting different results?

10. What are some examples of my obsessions today? Am I willing to see my ineffective, repetitive thoughts and behaviors as not sane?

11. Am I willing to believe there is a Power greater than myself? How do I notice that Power restoring me to sanity?

What It Looks Like

When I first came to the Twelve Steps I did not have a Higher Power. For me it was an evolution (one that is ongoing). I had to "act as if" in the beginning and ask for the willingness to come to believe. My sponsor said to start wherever I was, and that was what I did. In my journey, I read my Twelve-Step literature as well as the literature of a variety of spiritual traditions. I collected many different kinds of prayers, wrote some of my own, and spent many a night under the stars, asking this supposed Higher Power to help me.

I did not yet know if there really *was* a Higher Power, but my life had become so unmanageable, as I had discovered in Step One, that I was willing to do anything to get relief, to find some peace. I had nothing to lose, as I had lost it all, and I had everything to gain. For me, taking this Step came out of a place of despair and desperation.

~

This is lifelong work for me, and what I keep on discovering is that there are layers of insanity in me that seem to be revealed over time. At the same time, my Higher Power is more and more present in my life. For example, a week or so ago I had the experience of being very angry with someone, and I went to bed having obsessive thinking that kept me from sleeping. Finally, in a state of desperation, which is usually how it happens, I remembered to turn toward my Higher Power. I gave my anger to my Higher Power, and I fell asleep. In the morning, I was in a completely different state and able to make amends to this person. So to me, this is the realization of Step Two—having faith that my Higher Power can and will restore me to sanity if I only turn toward this Power greater than myself. It is a slow process, but feeling the miracle of it in my life brings me an ever-deepening belief that I will experience serenity and, one day at a time, become my best self.

~

I live with chronic pain and illness, and I need to be restored to sanity many times each day. I read this Step as part of a morning meditation each day, and I am OK for a while, then pain and fear come back *big time*. Sometimes I can get back on track after a little talk with my Higher Power. Sometimes I stop and read CPA literature. I need to remember this is a process, and I need to keep working at it. It is hard work for me.

I am not as depressed since finding this program. I have a strong spiritual base but not much emotional stability so far. I had surgery that had to be cancelled due to complications, and I still feel weak. They are going to reschedule the surgery, and I am not worried about it, but I'm fearful about my ability to recover from it. I turn this insanity over to my Higher Power for a while, and then I start the whole cycle of fear again. Then I do the first three Steps and get on with trying to live today. I am grateful to CPA for being here to show me the way.

~

Insanity for me was the desperation to keep up with everything, fulfilling everyone's expectations, the guilt for not doing so, the grief that I could not, the fear for what the future would hold, and the shame of letting people down. When I found CPA, a whole new world opened up to me, a world with hope for a good life in spite of my circumstances, and a world with tools both for practical application and for emotional and spiritual balance and serenity. I learn over and over again that my Higher Power can restore me to sanity.

When things are overwhelming, sometimes I remember to ask God to take this moment, this day, and to show me what is best for me. I turn the day over and rest in the knowledge that She is in control and that what needs to get done will get done, even if it is what I'm tempted to think of as "just resting." This brings me closer to sanity and farther from frustration and pain.

Another example is when I am feeling unusually good. When this happens, I want to do so much. I want to walk a lot farther when I go for my walk; I want to accomplish more; I want to take as few pain medications as I can, when I really might be better off taking my usual dose. In these instances, I am seeing that I also need to turn even these times over to God and ask for Her wisdom. If I don't, I get caught up in the insanity of pushing too hard and end up paying for it with more downtime and frustration.

~

For me, Spiritual Resources or Higher Powers are anything that feeds my humanity and nourishes my soul. Relying on them does not change physical outcomes but profoundly impacts my serenity and peace of mind and spirit. These resources are sort of "food" for the soul, and they take many different forms. I find my spiritual food in listening to my intuition (my Deeper Power); reading CPA literature; receiving the love and support of others at CPA; experiencing nature, magazines, photographs; turning to various religious leaders and using personal affirmations; writing myself letters from my Higher Power; praying; meditating; accepting others' love and the generosity of their time and friendship; and changing my thinking to softer, less critical, demanding thoughts.

Basically, anything that feels like Love, Understanding, Kindness or Forgiveness in that moment is my spiritual food. I can and do believe in these things because of the positive impact on my being. This relaxes my body and is wonderful for my total being in the world. I suppose you could say my Spiritual Resources are a verb—ever changing, teaching, loving, and inviting me to gently grow. Because these Steps refer to GOD, I use "Good Orderly Direction" to comprehend what that word means to me. It includes any resource that nurtures me and provides me with a quiet, accepting peace of mind.

~

Today I got some health news that scares me, overwhelms me, and just completely is freaking me out. It's a big thing and will dramatically affect my life. I am still feeling very nervous and scared. But I am trying to stay in the moment and not worry so much about the future and how this will affect it. Trying to stay in the present and do what I can do right now and give the rest over to my Higher Power is essential, because today my life feels very unmanageable.

Step Two—realizing that there is a Power greater than myself that can restore me to sanity—can lead me on the path I need to go. I can look at today and what I can do and let God worry about tomorrow. I am very weak. Very tired. I have no energy. So it seems there isn't much I can do in this moment. I will sit with God, wait to see what I can and can't do today, and stay within those parameters.

~

Step Two gently invites me to believe in something greater than my *self*. It teaches that it doesn't matter what form the greater Power takes, just so long as it is a Power that is not me—and I can wholeheartedly believe in it. Luckily, the Step also says we can take this piecemeal as we see fit. It took a long time of coming to the rooms and listening, searching, and seeking to develop my "evolving" deeper Power that I feel guided by, nurtured by, and loved by.

At first, I was stuck in the name game. Then I was tripped up by my childhood religious teachings; then I had a problem with trust. I did have a belief that there was a greater Power of some kind, but I never put in the time and effort to crystallize what it might offer. I tried on "other people's ideas" of their greater Power, but nothing fit just right.

I set down on paper what my greater Power would be if I in fact believed in one. I tried many times, but I was unsuccessful in finding a greater Power I could really believe in and trust. Because I was having such difficulty, I set this Step aside while I went on to the following Steps. I kept coming back to it, and kept coming back to it, and today I can say I have a greater Power in my life that I trust and who has relieved me of my confusion.

~

In the first part of the Step, I had to begin to redefine my sense of a Higher Power. I felt betrayed that all these health problems had happened to me. I am still redefining my sense of a Higher Power, and that will grow as I grow. My insanity was "I have to find a cure. I have to cure the symptoms."

Now in Step Two, I am letting go. I am letting go of the control I thought I had. I am beginning to develop a faith in something greater than myself. My insanity—I have it daily. This morning I woke up, felt crushing exhaustion, and wondered "how can I fix this?" Then I went about my self-care routine by opening my Step book as I ate breakfast. Step Two for me is a letting go and being open to faith and new possibilities.

~

I think the biggest insanity in my life around my issues in this arena is how I allow fear to control my every thought and action/inaction. Being restored to sanity means that I can live life more functionally than I have in the past. Before working the Steps, I was lying in bed, day after day, for fear of making my illness and pain worse if I did anything at all. For months, I was only doing the very bare minimum to exist. I've gone through this behavior many times in the past, and it's like being the walking dead.

Today, I can have pain sensations, observe illness symptoms, and walk through the day doing my activities anyway. I'm not doing as much as I used to do, but I'm doing and being—a step in the right direction. Today, thanks to the CPA Steps, I have found some acceptance in knowing that my symptoms come and go, are unpredictable, and sometimes unrelenting. I am learning that no matter how my body feels, I can be active, in moderation, often far more than my fearful brain believes I can.

Step Three

Made a decision to turn our will and our lives over to the care of God as we understood Him.

Ingredients

Humility
Willingness to give up self-will/self-centeredness
Letting go
Openness to Higher Power's will
Daily application
Faith

Description

Up to this point, we have made a series of decisions in our program: to come to meetings, to surrender, to accept the concept of a Higher Power. But these are not sufficient to bring about complete recovery from the effects of our pain and illness.

In the First Step we found the problem: that we were powerless and needed to surrender. In the Second Step we found the solution: in a Power greater than ourselves. In Step Three we start to *use* the solution: by turning our will and our lives over to the care of that Power.

Directions

We may be willing, after Step Two, to believe in a Power greater than ourselves. Now, are we willing to accept this solution: to be directed by our Higher Power? To do so, we need to become more fully aware of our self-will and how it keeps us closed off from our Higher Power.

Our life up until now has been based on self-will, and it has not been successful. We have tried to control people, places, and things, particularly our health and physical condition. These actions have not been effective. Our suffering is proof of this. Our self-centered way of operating has not brought us happiness.

The many people worldwide who have found recovery using the Twelve Steps have all come to the same conclusion.

Self-centeredness is the core of our problems. We thought we knew what was best for us, but things have not worked out. The antidote to our grandiosity is to surrender our will and put our Higher Power's plan first. We accept our true relationship to our Higher Power and others. We become rightsized. This is an exercise in humility. We take actions, and we leave the results to our Higher Power. We are unburdened of the responsibility of running the world.

We take Step Three by asking our Higher Power to relieve us of the "bondage of self" and to help us pray, "Thy will, not mine, be done."

We examine more fully our concept of a Higher Power, which is not defined for us by others. We continue to explore and arrive at an understanding of our own, which may change over time as our spiritual awareness deepens.

In this Step, we begin to see that the whole world does not revolve around us. We develop humility and maturity. We stop focusing only on what we think we need and want and shift our attention to what we can contribute to life. We learn to face life in new ways that bring peace, and our fears and anxieties begin to diminish. As we become aware of the realm of the spirit, our lives begin to change.

This is a Step we take daily. Every day we make the decision to turn over our will and life to the *care* of a loving Higher Power. We may do this in baby steps, but the important thing is to start to allow our Higher Power in. We open the door to hearing our Higher Power's guidance. Then we bring our thoughts, words, and actions into accordance with what we believe is our Higher Power's will for us. We do this by praying and meditating, talking with program friends, attending meetings, reading CPA literature, and relying on and practicing the Steps. The answers will appear.

Progress, not perfection, is our practice. When we get stuck or obstacles such as negative thinking interfere with our efforts, we acknowledge our powerlessness and ask our Higher Power to remove what is blocking our progress. We turn it over. Every day, we *Let Go and Let God*. We ask God to guide our thoughts, words, and actions and simply believe that once we have done so, we can count on the guidance we receive. This is how, one day at a time, we begin to rely on a Power greater than ourselves.

Some of us have a comfortable relationship with the Higher Power of our understanding. Some may have had negative experiences with religious organizations. CPA is not a religious program, but it is spiritual. Each member gets to define the terms of that spirituality for him- or herself and to find a personal relationship with a Power greater than oneself. This can be a truly exciting discovery. No matter who or what that Power is for us, our relationship with it is possibly the most intimate relationship we have ever had—one we know we can rely on.

We turn our pain and illness over to God without preconditions. We set no requirement for the outcome and do not ask for specific results. This would only be reaffirming our self-will. Instead, we turn the *outcome* over, accepting whatever the results may be. If we set a condition, we are limiting the outcome. Our Higher Power's outcomes may far exceed what we, left to our own minds and devices, can conceive. We humbly offer ourselves to this Power and put ourselves in its care.

One way to do this concretely is to create a "God Box" in which we write down our prayers and give God the situations that are troubling us. We may make a beautiful box, covered with images we love, or simply use a jar—any container that will hold little notes or tokens we put inside to represent our problems will do. Once we turn a situation over to God, we let go. We cannot set a time limit. Yet we may find ourselves taking it back. Again, we let it go. If we do find ourselves being impatient, wanting to force a solution of our own, we repeat the process and let it go, as many times as necessary.

Our self-reliance and determination have not served us well in living with chronic pain and illness. It is worth trying something different. We are already at our worst, so we have nothing more to lose. We have lost so much already.

In this Step, we don't have to do anything but make the decision to turn our will and our lives over to our Higher Power's care. This does not solve all our problems. It opens the door for help and makes it possible for us to step out of the way.

We can enjoy this process. When we make this decision, small and large moments of recovery start to happen, and we begin to trust that we will be guided and cared for. We are no longer in charge. We place ourselves in capable hands. Daily, we set aside our willfulness and determination to be right and believe that our Higher Power will guide us in the best direction. It is time to cease being the pilot and become the copilot in our life. We yield to our Higher Power navigating our way.

We believe our Higher Power does not want us to just barely survive and exist. When we really let go, it becomes clear: our Higher Power wants us to be free from despair, to thrive, and to have a full, rewarding life. Making this decision in Step Three gives us faith that this is so.

Working the Step

1. In what ways do I cling to my self-will? How well has this worked for me?

2. What blocks me from surrendering to the God of my understanding? What is needed to remove the blocks?

3. How can I apply Step Three even if I don't have a Higher Power of my own?

4. Do I trust my Higher Power to care for me? If not, what holds me back? Have I considered asking my Higher Power for help to remove my concerns?

5. What does it mean to me to "let go"? How do I understand the slogan *Let Go and Let God*?

6. Am I willing to turn to a Higher Power, daily, for guidance? If not, what is in the way? What would have to change?

7. In what ways do I seek my Higher Power's guidance?

8. How do I recognize God's will from my own?

9. In what ways does Step Three ease my fears?

10. What is my resistance to turning my will over? What will help me make the decision?

11. What has happened when I have turned over my will to a Higher Power of my understanding?

12. What prompts me to take my will back? How do I know when I have done so? What tools will help me when I "take it back"?

13. Am I ready to make the decision to turn over my will?

What It Looks Like

I feel the biggest change in my life from the Twelve Steps has been the ability to turn things over. This is a huge change. I see how much energy, stress, and worry I free myself from when I trust in my Higher Power and just do my footwork.

An example is that I recently got one of those review letters from Social Security. I was filling out the information, and I contacted my physician to let her know and ask for her support. Now I know you don't know me, but in the past I would have been freaking out: so afraid something was going to happen or go wrong, worried about what the doctor wrote, stressing out about losing my benefits, worrying about how I am going to survive, and on and on. I can't tell you how much stress, worry, negative energy and thoughts I would have generated. I am amazed at how I am now handling it.

I know I am disabled and unable to work, because if there was a way I could make more money, I guarantee I would be working. I have an active medical history, and I communicate with my doctors. This is the big one: I know that my Higher Power is going to take care of me, so all I have to do is my part and then turn it over. Now I know some people would say, "What's the big deal?" I was *incapable* of letting go of obsessive and irrational worry in the past. I am so grateful for the miracle and the relief it brings to have faith in a Higher Power.

~

I remember hearing once at a meeting that "our will and our lives" were equivalent to our thoughts and our actions. I try to remember that and think about it, because it helps me understand what the Step is saying. I have to hear and see examples of this in order to understand. That's why I have to listen to other people's stories of success. That's when I can get inspired.

But I have to make a conscious effort, and sometimes it's really hard because I can't see the outcome; I guess that's why they call it faith. When I look back, it always seems to pay off in peace and serenity. Lately it's been when I'm in pain, thinking that *this too shall pass,* and sometimes my action is to do nothing or do something easy, which is contrary to what I've done in the past. It used to be that I had to push myself; now it's to take it easy and do things when I'm up to it. It's deeper, and it's about being more humble and asking for help. I'll keep coming back.

~

One thing I didn't turn over for a long time, and was in self-will about, was my ability to work. Being in denial, I was making myself sicker by trying to work. Then something happened at work that aggravated my illness, and I wanted my employer to accommodate me. I got sicker every day. I wanted a particular result—that my employer would accommodate me so I could continue at my job.

Then I did something different, and I prayed a lot about it and turned over my will. When I turned it over, something happened that I could never imagine. I was given six months off with pay to get my treatment. This was a totally unexpected outcome of my decision to turn over my will and my life. I could not have imagined that result, so there is no way I could have made it happen or even asked for it. It was hard to have confidence in my Higher Power, but I am so grateful I did it.

~

I love the line "You can't expect different results doing the same thing over and over." The shift that occurs in Step Three is surrendering our control over to God. We no longer believe we are in charge and that we have all the answers. This change in perspective allows for new possibilities to occur in our lives. My understanding of God is a relationship, and like all relationships, as I change so does that relationship.

In the beginning of learning this Step, I read spiritual books, asked questions of others, found myself revisiting the religion of my childhood, and spent a lot of time in nature. There are peaceful, beautiful trails around my house, and when I had the energy to be outside, I'd talk to God on my hikes. If you'd seen me at that time you'd have thought I was the crazy lady talking to herself. At night, under the blanket of stars, I'd lie in the grass in my backyard and have long talks with God. These days I have a place in my house where I meditate, and that is often where I go to speak, and more important, to listen to my Higher Power.

As a result of practicing Step Three, I recognize my life is in the care of God. I don't need to worry about the future, to figure things out, or to manage anything other than what is before me in this moment. I forget often and find myself trying to plan and predict, as though I have control over what will happen during the coming days and months of my life. Then I read this Step and remember again that all is well under the loving care of God.

∼

Unfortunately, my image of God was of a fearful God who could punish me and even send me to hell for all eternity. This concept of God was also clouded by my church's teachings regarding homosexuality. I am a gay man. So when I came to these Twelve Steps and you told me that I could have my own personal understanding of what God meant to me, I found that attractive. It was a process to come to this understanding. Eventually, I came to believe that my God is an all-loving and all-forgiving God and that He loves me always. This understanding makes it so much easier to put my life and my will (I say my thoughts and my actions) in the "care" of my God.

And remember, Step Three says, "Made a decision to . . .," so at first I am just making the decision. I pray for the willingness to complete that action. In my daily life, this means that I ask my God to guide my thinking and my actions for the day. And when I come to points in my day where I face uncertainty or indecision, I try to stop, pause, and ask God for direction. Do I do this always? Nope, sure don't! I'm human, and I make mistakes and I forget. But Step Three is something I try to do and practice whenever I can.

∼

I have a bowl in my bedroom. Whatever I need to let go of, I write it on a piece of paper and put it in the bowl. It is out of my hands. This helps me let go of it.

∼

My understanding of God has morphed into many different versions over time, and even today, it is not solid and set in stone. It is a fluid understanding. The more I experience my Higher Power, the more is revealed to me. For this I am grateful.

∼

Over the past several days, I've been turning to my Higher Power like a moth to a flame. Yesterday, I asked my Higher Power to give me results that were benign concerning my breast biopsies. Well, this morning I got my results. One is benign. The other isn't. I have breast cancer. I am still processing this. I think I'm in shock. At this point, I've been told that a surgeon will call to set up an appointment to discuss my options. I've spoken to a close friend who had a double mastectomy this summer, and she has been helping me put this into some perspective. This isn't going to kill me, or so I've been told. Whatever it does or doesn't do, I don't want any more pain. That is the thing I'm most scared of. I have so many feelings about this right now: anger, sadness, loss, victimization. I keep thinking, "Don't I have enough to deal with without this?"

Little by little, I'm becoming aware that I'm thinking about this in a way that would have been different without CPA. While I feel all these darker feelings, I also feel held—held in the thoughts of those who love me and care for me. Tonight, my son was talking about how crappy the last year has been. His dad died last March, and he is trying to write a dissertation. He said, "No matter what, Mom, you're my priority." I get it. He doesn't want to lose his last parent, but I also get how much he loves me. When I joined CPA over two years ago, I wasn't sure about that. I tended to deny or devalue other people's love for me. I called my brother, who lives far away and whom I only talk to three times yearly. He said, "When do you want me to come out there?" That blew my mind. He has never offered to visit to take care of me in all the time I've been ill. Just those two people, among others who I know will have my back, are making me feel a whole lot safer and cared for.

At the beginning of the week, after the biopsies, I couldn't think straight about what would happen if I got this diagnosis. My CPA group helped me to think about how I didn't need to know. I need to turn it over and help will arrive. I know it is here and it is on its way.

~

My pain doctor screwed up and forgot to have the medications he told me would be available so that the procedure would go easier and be more peaceful. It got very painful and claustrophobic on that table. I was awake and afraid I'd strangle on my spit, which was collecting in my throat for the hour and a half that I was cautioned to be still. If I moved a muscle, the needle wouldn't go to the right location, they wouldn't get the necessary sample, and I'd just have to be there longer, in greater pain.

I began to have a mini panic attack, and all of a sudden I thought, "Higher Power. I need to turn to my Higher Power." Right then, I took the smallest breath possible and prayed for help getting through it. I felt a sense of comfort and a feeling of settling in, just being there, experiencing everything that was happening— still painful but with a lot less fear. I knew I could make it with the help of my Higher Power, which was given through a feeling of calm and serenity.

Sometimes when things get rough, I forget to turn to my Higher Power. On this day I remembered, and my Higher Power was there.

Step Four

Made a searching and fearless moral inventory of ourselves.

Ingredients

Praying for the courage, guidance, and willingness to work
   the Step
Sponsor—not doing it alone
Honesty
Trust—that this is the path to a new and better future
Nonjudgmental approach
Desire for self-knowledge
Written inventory
Identifying fears and resentments
Inclusion of liabilities and assets

Description

Step Four is a rigorous inventory of what is on the "shelves" of our inner storehouse of personal characteristics. We become familiar with our liabilities and assets—the patterns and habits that shape our character and motivate our daily thoughts and behaviors. We are able to do this inventory fearlessly, with the foundation of a strong relationship with a Power greater than ourselves, who is guiding and supporting us.

Directions

Before we begin, we pray for the courage and guidance we need; we may even put a prayer for our Fourth Step in our God Box. It is strongly suggested that no one work the Steps alone and certainly to have the help and support of a sponsor while working Step Four. With prayer, and with our sponsor supporting us, we trust that we will receive all we need to work this Step, and we begin.

This inventory is similar to a business inventory; it is a fact-finding mission to discover what we have stocked. We don't judge what we find. No item is good or bad; we are merely making an accounting of what is there. We become aware of what works well for us and what no longer serves us in a beneficial way.

When we do our inventory, it needs to be fearless searching and entirely honest. It is possible we may uncover secrets that have been holding us hostage. In this Step, we can be liberated from the baggage of the past. Some of us have never taken a serious and complete look at ourselves, and in doing this Step, we discover ourselves for the first time.

There is no right or wrong way to take the inventory. We need to find what works best for us. By doing an online search, we can also find checklists available that offer suggestions of traits that we may find in our inventory. For the inventory itself, some people use a method that involves making columns. In these columns, they list who and what they hold negative feelings about. Another method is to look back over your life in five-year increments and simply write about any unfinished business you have with people, places, and events—anything that still troubles you. Your sponsor can help guide you in choosing a nonjudgmental and effective approach. There are several suggested formats for Step Four in Appendix A of this book.

It is important that this Step is written out. We can look at the inventory through the lens of assets and liabilities or as strengths and weaknesses. Some items might fit into more than one category: an asset, taken to an extreme, can become a liability. We can write our inventory out in whatever way works for us to see it most clearly. The objective is to be honest and to get a full picture of ourselves—how we think, how we act, how we speak, how we treat ourselves and others. We may want to keep our written list in a safe place. Later, in our Eighth and Ninth Steps, this list will help us identify where we need to make amends.

In our inventory, we bring everything out into the light, and we examine it. Then we can decide what has helped us and what has hurt us. We want to look at resentments, fears, and pride. When have we felt shame, righteousness, guilt, and indignation?

Where have we been dishonest? Where have we had courage? We note what is of benefit and what is toxic. We need to be thorough and do our best to not leave anything out. We look at the ways we have hurt ourselves and others, at the places that scare us, and at how we have created narratives that keep us imprisoned in a world of hurt. It may be daunting, but it is necessary to have a clear vision of where we are.

Importantly, we are taking our *own* inventory, not that of others. There is no blaming and no shaming in this process. Holding on to grudges, real or imagined, means that others are controlling our lives. Whether it's health-care providers, insurance companies, or lack of support and understanding from friends and family, it will free us if we let go of our resentments. They are causing us emotional pain and keeping us stuck in the past.

With a clear picture of ourselves, we can identify old habits that may have served a purpose at one time, possibly to keep us safe, but which are no longer effective and may even be harmful today. We are seeking freedom in this Step. The liberation that comes from exposing our negative thoughts and behaviors is great, and it provides the hope and possibility for change.

Our inventory will not be complete if it does not include everything that is on our shelves. Many people think they are finished when they have listed what they perceive as their negative traits. It is crucial that we do an inventory that includes all aspects of us, which means listing the areas in which we have strengths, areas in which we have made positive choices in our lives, and ways we have contributed to the world. Balance is vital in this Step, and it is part of being honest.

When we are done, we will have a list of characteristics— thought and behavior patterns, relationships, and events—that make us who we are today. We will learn things we may have missed seeing in the past, talents we have not noticed, as well as shame and secrets long ago hidden away. We become aware of the places in which we are blocked from Spirit—the ways in which we cloaked parts of ourselves in darkness, where they could not be healed. We see clearly where we are still living in the problems, so that we can begin to live in the solutions.

We do this without judgment. We bring light into all the dark corners and clear out all the cobwebs. We open windows and bring in fresh air. All can become new and revitalized.

We have not always been honest or realistic. We imagine that if our pain and illness disappeared overnight, so would all our problems. However, many of our problems were with us before we became afflicted, and it can be a surprise to realize that they won't go away even if the pain and illness do. In this program of letting go and of action, the fearless and moral inventory is a step toward our emotional and spiritual restoration.

With clarity about who we have been and who we are now, seeing what is no longer of benefit and what assists us, we begin to head in a new direction. We become willing to let go of those aspects that no longer serve a purpose in our life and ask for guidance in how to respond wisely going forward.

As with all the Steps, we can spend as much time as we need on this one. It won't be done perfectly, and that is OK. We just need to complete it. Many of us find that, after a few years, if we do another Step Four we discover we can go deeper and are able to see much more. Each time we come back and work this Step again, we learn more about ourselves. This is a Step in learning to love ourselves fully, just as we are, in this moment.

Working the Step

1. What prevents me from doing this Step? What would help me find the willingness to work this Step?

2. What makes it a moral inventory?

3. What stands in the way of my working this Step honestly?

4. Have I asked my Higher Power for support and guidance? Have I asked others in the program to help me?

5. In what ways do my secrets interfere with my recovery?

6. Have I included strengths and assets in my inventory?

7. In what ways does denial maintain my negative thoughts and behaviors?

8. Are there assets or virtues I am afraid to admit are mine?

9. How does it feel to discover the specifics of my own participation in my difficulties? What do I get from denying it? What do I get from accepting it?

10. Is my inventory fearless and searching, including all my secrets?

11. How do I feel now that my inventory is thoroughly completed?

What It Looks Like

Step Four is the first of six action Steps. I started this Step of reviewing my past life by looking at my assets and liabilities. It was vital to work the Step with my sponsor, who guided, supported, and encouraged me as I moved forward through the process. I thought this would be a difficult Step, but there really are no "must dos," and I was told there is no set length of time to complete it. My sponsor suggested I not rush to finish it quickly and reminded me to take my time and relax, to not get stressed out. I found that when I was gentle and kind with myself, placed no demands on myself to "conquer" the Step, the information I sought showed up with ease.

$\sim$

As a result of doing Step Four, I've woken up to new perspectives. Basically, in CPA I am recovering from the obsession over my pain and my body. There are times I've had a belief of entitlement due to my pain and illness. There is no way I could have looked at the painful truth of my negative thoughts and behaviors in Step Four without the strong foundation of the first three Steps and the faith in a Higher Power who loves me, sees the best in me, and wants the best for me.

In the past, when I saw something about myself I didn't like, I played an old tape that said, "You are worthless, and your life has no value." With help from my sponsor and friends in the fellowship, I can recognize the harsh voice that runs in my head and work the next Steps without the denigrating, false messages from my childhood. Instead of being stuck in the dark cave of self-pity for weeks or months, I can start to see the best in myself.

~

As I investigated Step Four, I was surprised to discover that I wasn't always kind to others, or to myself, and had used my pain and illness as a "Get Out of Jail Free" card more times than I wished to admit. I learned that many of the things I accused others of were also behaviors that I engaged in. If it weren't for the support of my sponsor, my friends, and the love of my Higher Power, I would have felt overwhelmed by the guilt and shame that showed up as I became more aware of my past words and actions.

~

Owning the strengths in my inventory was a hard part of this Step for me. It was a challenge when I feel like so much was taken away with my illness. I was able to see that there were still parts of me intact. I learned in CPA that my Higher Power loves me just as I am. This Step was the beginning of learning how to love myself just as I am today.

~

Looking ahead to this Step filled me with reluctance. I thought it was going to be a case of declaring my past "bad" deeds and admitting all my negative qualities. It seemed like a lot of unpleasant work and very time consuming. Boy was I wrong! The result of completing Step Four was a comfortable knowing and acceptance of myself, strengths and weaknesses, and a continuous awareness of when my defects of character were not serving me.

~

The Fourth Step can seem overwhelming at first, but taking it slow is the key. You just have to begin and put into practice *Easy Does It*.

Yesterday I was in a difficult personal interaction with my physical therapist. As an attempt to smooth over what could have become an escalating situation, I injected some off-the-wall humor to make her laugh, hence turning a bad situation into a laughing matter. This is something I do well. Humor is an asset I wrote down as a strength in my inventory.

Today I became impatient with my son (which happens all too often), and that incident highlighted my impatience and tendency to be quick to anger. These were written down (in my inventory) as things to improve. I like to keep it positive, so I don't write "defects" but "things to improve."

~

When I was fearless in my Step Four in CPA, I discovered that I had always believed that I was the one who endured all the suffering. I didn't realize how much pain my illness and behavior caused those close to me. When I am ill, I can get "irritable and unreasonable." I expect everyone else to accommodate my needs and make me comfortable. Doing my Step Four helped me to see that I could be demanding and insensitive to the needs of others. This Step sets the groundwork for later Steps in which we make amends. I began to see around the blind spots that were created by my illness. It is so easy to expect the focus to be on me when I am not well.

∽

Step Four helps me to see the essence of who I am—my gifts and my character defects. It is a way of stepping back and seeing myself as I am today and letting go of the me I used to be before I became ill. It is a time to remember that my Higher Power does not make junk. In Step Four, I learned I am a worthwhile human being, not because of what I accomplish but because I exist. God loves me even on the days I never leave my bed.

Step Five

Admitted to God, to ourselves, and to another human being the exact nature of our wrongs.

Ingredients

Courage
Rigorous honesty
Attention to patterns
Forgiveness
Humility
Trust
Confidentiality
Acceptance
"We"

Description

In Step Five, we declare what we learned in Step Four to a compassionate Higher Power and to ourselves. However, we must also share what we have written with another person. We are never alone in our program, and confiding our list with a trusted friend makes it clear to us that we are not unique and that others have had similar behaviors and experiences. Not only is this a relief, it empowers us to move forward, giving us hope that change is possible.

In doing this Step, we are being honest with God, with ourselves, and with another person. We are practicing trust in another human being and forgiveness of ourselves. These actions are important so we can become unburdened of all the pain we carry in our mind, heart, and body.

Directions

The first two parts of this Step may seem unnecessary. Don't we already know what we uncovered in our Step Four inventory? And didn't our Higher Power already know these things, even before we did? Nonetheless, we trust those who have walked this path before us, and we start with our Higher Power. When we take the time to "talk" to our Higher Power (in formal prayer or whatever form of communication feels real to us) and admit the "exact nature of our wrongs," we create a connection with our Higher Power that is personal. We are specific and fully honest. Trust in our Higher Power as our friend and confidante grows, and we develop courage knowing we are no longer alone. This is the beginning of forgiveness and becoming liberated from the past.

When we admit what we have uncovered to ourselves, by talking to our reflection in a mirror, perhaps, or writing an entry in a journal, our relationship with ourselves becomes revitalized. We have identified what's been holding us back, and we are sincere in our efforts to have a different kind of life. This is the beginning of a new self-respect. We no longer need to hide the shame of our "wrongs." With our Higher Power supporting us, the willingness to face ourselves, and the ability to safely acknowledge the details of our lives, we are ready to admit them to another person.

Since we live with chronic pain and illness and our energy can be limited, our ability to focus can also be hampered; it may be that we do our Step Four and Step Five over an extended period of time. We can start our inventory, share what we have learned with our sponsor, and then continue working on it. It may take several meetings to complete Step Five.

It may be frightening to think of admitting all our personal information to someone else. In taking this Step, we learn that our past is not as bad as we think and that there are others who will care about us unconditionally, even when they know the worst about us. Since some of us enter into this Step feeling fear, it is helpful to say the Serenity Prayer before beginning. We may wish to take a moment of silent meditation and prayer. We ask our Higher Power for strength and courage.

We diligently did our fact-finding mission in Step Four, and now we share what we discovered. This takes courage, but knowing that all others who have walked the path of the Twelve Steps have done this, to great healing effect, gives us the confidence we need.

We choose to share the intimate details of our life with our sponsor. We have some trust by now with our sponsor, and although it may seem formidable, we know we can confide safely in him or her.

Or, we may wish to share our Fifth Step with a clergy member, spiritual guide or therapist, or someone else in recovery. This Step calls for a gentle, loving witness to our spiritual journey. It is important this is someone who is caring and nonjudgmental and who will respect our confidentiality. If not our sponsor, it is a good idea to choose someone who is familiar with Twelve-Step recovery, but this is not required. It is important, however, to choose someone who is not a relative or close friend who may have been personally affected by our past attitudes and behaviors.

This is a Step in trust and humility. Unless we share our inventory, we may deceive ourselves. We confide in another person who has traveled this same territory so that they can help us see who we really are. It is never as bad or as good as we thought. We are all humans, doing the best we can. By sharing this inventory with another person, we are no longer living alone in the dark. In Step Four, we have illuminated every room in our inner house. Every nook and cranny is exposed and known, sometimes for the first time. Some are pleasant surprises, while others are shocking. Humility is both a necessary ingredient in taking Step Five and one of its richest rewards.

Sharing how we came to be in our current relationship with life, including our chronic pain and chronic illness, being rigorously honest and open about the causes and situations we have discovered, demystifies our past. It gives the past far less power over us than it has had up until now. It reduces our shame. Shame only has power over us when our past is kept hidden. Once our secrets are exposed, they no longer control us.

Sharing with another person who is a mirror for us helps us see ourselves clearly, rather than through our own distorted vision.

It is quite common, in fact, for our trusted witness to smile and let us know that they themselves have behaved similarly. We are seen, we are understood, we feel forgiven, and we are able to forgive.

Looking at the wreckage of the past honestly and completely, we can identify what we need to let go of so we can start fresh. Seeing our attributes, we can see our humanity—we are neither all bad nor all good. We begin to rightsize our perception of ourselves.

We do all this in the loving presence of another person and our Higher Power. We don't judge ourselves and neither does our listener. We take all the time we need, in a private, safe setting, possibly over several meetings, in order to share it all and feel complete. Together, we identify repetitive patterns of thinking and behavior that do not serve us well. We look at past errors and find their true causes. We see our talents, strengths, and positive attributes. We begin to see ourselves through new eyes. We find the best in ourselves and build on that.

When we are done, we have a list of our assets and defects of character. These are what we will bring forward into Step Six and Step Seven. This list will continue to be a useful tool when we begin Steps Eight, Nine, and Ten.

Step Five is a privilege both to share and to hear. As the person we confide in listens, they are reminded of their own assets and liabilities—and their own potential for growth. It is a time of openness, trust, and kindness between us, our listener, and our Higher Power. In Step Five, the "we" aspect of this program becomes crystal clear: we truly are in this together.

Once we have taken Step Five, we can move forward in awareness. There is no longer any vagueness, any confusion, or finger-pointing to those outside of ourselves. This is the beginning of a new way of life. We already know a life of discontentment, irritability, anger, and aloneness. We are moving into freedom, into a life far more beautiful than we thought possible.

Working the Step

1. Why is humility necessary in this Step?

2. What has kept me from trusting others and being willing to open myself up?

3. How has sharing honestly helped me recover from the emotional pain I've experienced?

4. Was there anything I held back sharing? What was in the way of talking about it? Can I ask for the willingness to share it so that I can be free of all my secrets?

5. In what ways does this Step release me from shame?

6. What patterns of thinking and behavior have I recognized in doing this Step?

7. What fears showed up in doing this Step?

8. What resentments did I discover?

9. Was I willing to include my assets in my inventory? Was I willing to share them?

10. Do I feel less isolated after doing this Step? How do I know I am "in it together" with others, in my life and in this program?

11. Have I made a list of character assets and a list of defects to bring to Steps Six and Seven to use in my Step work going forward?

What It Looks Like

Working a Fourth and Fifth Step with my sponsor helped me out so much. It transformed me. I was so angry about my illness and all the doctors and all the specialists and the way that friends and family reacted to my illness. So much of it was a very negative experience for me. I was carrying that anger and frustration and sadness; it was exacerbating my symptoms, and I had no peace.

After writing it all down thoroughly in the Fourth Step, and then going over it all with my sponsor in the Fifth Step, I was able to gain a better perspective about it all: the doctors, the medical system, insurance companies, government policies, specialists, you name it. All of it.

I began to see my part in it and was able to take responsibility for my part, thereby no longer being such a victim of my own chronic pain and illness. Working Steps Four and Five changed my life for the better, even though my circumstances and health were the same.

~

This Step helped me let go of shame I had about being ill. At some subconscious level, there was a belief that I brought this on myself, that I deserved it, that I was no longer as good as people who were well.

In sharing my Step Four with my sponsor, I discovered that what I was experiencing was shared by others. I found that I was not deficient or inadequate as a human being just because I had an illness. I reconnected with the truth. I am lovable just because I am alive. I don't have to do or be anything to know I am worthy of love and respect, from myself and others.

Some of the discoveries that I revealed were related to how I dealt with my illness. There were times I was so angry at healthy people and their inability to understand me. I often felt like I was disdained, or ignored, or treated with disregard. It was often my projection and not the truth. Out of my own suffering, I would read things into the actions and words of others that were not based in reality. In my anger, I would wish some people to be ill like me so they would know how much I suffered.

There were times I enjoyed all the attention I received, a bit too much, and would dramatize my condition to get more sympathy. I would use my illness as an excuse for things I didn't want to do. I would use my illness to excuse behaviors that were not nice or kind. I was insensitive to the needs of family and friends because I was the one suffering and needed more than they did. I was selfish and self-centered at times because I thought that illness gave me the license to be so. I treated health-care personnel rudely when they didn't meet my expectations. I sometimes acted like a demanding child, and no one could say anything about it because I was ill and they didn't dare.

Not pretty. Doing Steps Four and Five made it possible to begin to clean the wreckage of the past and take responsibility for my attitude, my behavior, and my relationships with others. It helped me begin to heal my spirit and become a whole human being regardless of how my body functioned. It helped me start to love myself, just as I was, perfectly imperfect.

∼

For my Step Four I wrote my life history, and then when it was time for Step Five, I felt nervous about sharing it. I didn't know if I could talk about my chronic pain and my sexual history. I was raped, and I knew my sponsor didn't have the same experience as me. I was considering doing parts of Step Five with someone else. I prayed about it a lot and did my Fifth Step—even shared experiences my sponsor and I don't have in common—with her. It was liberating. My sponsor came to my house, and I read my Fourth Step history. I thought it would feel shameful to read to her. How would she look at me afterwards? Then I remembered that all I had gotten from her until this point was love, unconditional support, and compassion.

I learned in this Step that the human feelings of suffering, whatever the cause of the suffering, are universal. My sponsor didn't have to understand by sharing the same experiences as me. All she had to do was listen without judgment and be loving and supportive. I felt safe sharing my life story with her and was able to love myself a bit more.

~

Issues concerning my behavior while under the influence of pain had to be addressed. I had become incredibly difficult to live with, causing everyone around me to "walk on eggshells." My family would almost duck for cover when they saw me coming. It was apparent that I had an incredible amount of anger simmering under the surface, and it was only a matter of time before I blew again.

So I had to look at my anger, what I had become, and the damage I had caused to my marriage and to my family. I *had* to get real. My wife and I went to couples' counseling for the first time in seventeen years. And I had to force myself to sit and listen as I heard about the tyrant I had become. And I had to admit to my wife, to the therapist, and my God what a terrible person I had become. And then I went on to work the rest of the Steps around the anger issue and others.

Today, I am working with my CPA sponsor and focusing on the other issues that need to be addressed, such as fear, grief, and so on. I am also working with my sponsor to do my Fifth Step in parts. I e-mail her when I am finished with one part of my Fourth Step, then we go over it together. I found that this makes it all seem a bit less overwhelming.

It has been very liberating to uncover these "challenges" of character, share them, and then turn them over to my Higher Power. Today I am no longer ruled by my anger, and I am able to make that energy work for me in a more positive way.

~

I was dealing with shame, but I also was beginning to relish being a victim. *How great is it to discover a tumor inside my spinal cord that ends up paralyzing me? Now isn't that the perfect condition for people to feel sorry for me, to make me the center of attention, to want to help and come up to me at each occasion to ask how I am doing? Oh, how sad this is.*

Well, I got hooked into this "victim thing" very quickly! I had lived being a victim for most of my drinking years. I knew how damaging this can be. When I did my Fifth Step with my sponsor, I quickly came to see how my actions had brought about these two conditions of victimhood and shame. I could see how I felt ashamed of myself. I felt like a lesser human being for how I had left my family without one of its wage earners. I felt like a lesser human being for being so dependent on other people for basic conditions. I couldn't drive; someone else had to drive me. I wasn't able to control my bladder and bowels consistently. I couldn't walk. I really got down on myself, and I was dealing with depression, too.

When I shared my deepest secrets with another human being, those secrets I have held for years and didn't want anyone at any time to know about me; when I took those off my shoulders, It was truly liberating. When I told my sponsor, "I really wish Mr. X was paralyzed just like me, then *he* would know how I feel," or about how I had stolen some coins from my grandmother when I was nine years old and had never told anyone—that was liberating. When I can get these things off my chest and stop feeling shame about these simple little actions from my past, I can become free to deal honestly with who I am today.

When I worked with my sponsor to see how being a victim was no longer serving me (it actually never did serve me), then I could move on to a healthier way of interacting with others, coming from strength. I couldn't have done this without working the Fourth and Fifth Steps.

~

Step Five gave me the opportunity to share my personal life story with another person, my sponsor. By this time we had established a positive, caring relationship in which I felt safe and ready to trust him.

The other relationship I brought into this Step with me was the loving and forgiving God of my understanding. In Steps One, Two, and Three, the spiritual aspects of the program were emphasized. Now I continued to bring the spiritual connection with my "loving God" into this Step and all those that followed.

It's my belief that having a personal relationship with my God helped me immensely as I proceeded on my journey to accomplish the Steps. When I personalize my relationship with my Higher Power, it gives me a strong connection. It is comforting to know I am not alone. This relationship is there twenty-four hours a day. When I am in pain, I know I am being cared for when I feel this closeness to my Higher Power.

Step Six

*Were entirely ready to have God
remove all these defects of character.*

Ingredients

List of liabilities (defects of character)
Willingness
Acceptance
Giving up of self-will
Prayer
Trust in our Higher Power
Humility
Patience
Faith

Description

In Steps Four and Five, we identified aspects of our personalities that are troublesome. We now want to be relieved of these shortcomings, hopefully as soon as possible. Yet in Step Six, we are told that we cannot make them go away on our own. We must become ready to have them removed. This is the Step in which we accept a true partnership with a Power greater than ourselves. With our Higher Power's help, we can overcome our obstacles, and miracles can grace our lives. Serenity can replace despair. In this Step, we use our defects of character to deepen our faith. We no longer need to struggle alone.

Directions

Are we willing to behave differently than we have in the past? Are we willing to change and be changed? These are simple questions, and they can be answered with either yes or no. And so this Step seems as though it is quite easy; perhaps it will take no time at all. We merely need to answer these questions affirmatively. The fact that there is a Step Six on the path to recovery indicates that this task takes particular attention. It suggests that not only do we need to be willing but we need to become *ready* to change.

Along the path of the Twelve Steps, our readiness to move to the next Step is often indicated by our level of acceptance. Our part in working this Step is to accept ourselves as we are—defects of character and all. We also accept that we are not in charge and that we trust the Power that is. When we say yes to all this, we become ready and willing to let go of all that stands in the way of our physical, emotional, and spiritual well-being. We open the door to new possibilities.

We bring our list of character defects to the foreground. These are the obstacles to our forward motion. Are we truly willing and ready to let them go? For some of them, we will answer a resounding yes. For example, we are quite ready to have our dramatic tone of suffering removed. But what about our sense of superiority or inferiority? Are we ready to let that go? There may be character defects that we feel define us. Even these we are asked to become ready to have removed. Some may have shielded or protected painful realities. We have recognized that they are in our way to true freedom and happiness, but it can be hard to really let them go. Luckily, we do not have to remove them ourselves! Nor can we.

We leave the removal of these obstacles up to our Higher Power. All we need do is to become ready for our Higher Power to do so. We do this by no longer trying to fix ourselves, by interrupting our tendency to stay focused on our troubles, and by knowing we can trust our Higher Power.

If we find ourselves insisting on our way once again, we try to see where our resistance is coming from and pray for the willingness to let it go. This takes patience and forgiveness and reminds us of the necessity of humility.

We strive for the ideal of being *entirely ready* and are careful not to be too hard on ourselves when we fall short. Beating ourselves up is part of the old pattern that brought us to where we are; it invites our belief that we are in charge and that if we just punish ourselves enough we can fix things—we can be perfect. Perfection is not our goal. Trusting our Higher Power is.

We practice forgiveness and acceptance of ourselves as we progress forward. We pray for the willingness we need. We are learning how to let go of survival skills that no longer serve our best welfare. This takes patience. The Twelve Steps, the fellowship, and our Higher Power will do for us what we cannot do for ourselves. Step Six deepens our faith that this is so.

In Step Seven, we will ask our Higher Power to remove whatever is in the way of being of maximum service. We ask for clarity and strength. In Step Six, however, we simply decide to trust our Higher Power with this task. We let go fully of what we thought was our job and get ready to have our liabilities, all that blocks our serenity and joy, removed.

Becoming entirely ready may happen incrementally, but with every yes we say to letting go of our defects, we are taking a giant step in the direction of true freedom.

Working the Step

1. Did I make a clear list of the defects of character discovered in Steps Four and Five?

2. Did I pray for the willingness to be ready to have them removed? If not, what will help me do so?

3. What prevents me from being entirely ready for God to remove my defects of character?

4. What does readiness mean to me? How do I become ready?

5. Have I accepted my defects? If not, what is in my way?

6. How will my life look different if these defects of character are removed?

7. Am I afraid to have certain defects removed? Which ones? What am I afraid will happen?

8. How might removal of these defects of character restore me to sanity?

9. Do I understand I can't do this myself, that I need my Higher Power?

10. How will I put this Step into action?

11. In what ways do I trust the God of my understanding?

12. How does the Serenity Prayer help me with this Step?

What It Looks Like

When I got to Step Six I was able, with great relief and satisfaction, to turn to the God of my understanding. I was ready to let go of all the misery and suffering, all that impeded my recovery and a life that I enjoyed. I was so ready. I had dealt with pain my whole life in different ways and different areas. I had dealt with the same issues, again and again, and a recent geographic relocation wasn't changing anything. I could not deal with this my entire life. I was ready to let go. I was ready to be renewed.

In many ways my life was stuck, with me as a sixteen-year-old boy. I never matured from those days. By working the Steps, I was able to move on. The world has been wonderful since then. I've had challenges come my way, but I have been able to deal with them. As a result of doing the Steps, I like who I am today, and I like my life. I feel like I got to start over, that I am renewed. Step Six was the start of this process.

~

When I first approached Step Six, I was not immediately ready to have God remove my shortcomings. So for me, the Sixth Step is about willingness. After working my Fourth and Fifth Steps, I have a list of unhealthy thoughts and behaviors that need to be addressed. I can see how these flaws in my character have not served me and that I need to let them go. But I am not always willing to do so. When I have resistance to letting go of a behavior or a belief, I remain stuck. Even when it is clear that a certain behavior isn't good for me, I still tend to hold on.

Change often requires energy I don't want to expend. So what I do today is pray for the willingness to let go. I have found repeatedly that this does work. Each time I ask my Higher Power for the willingness to do things differently, I become a bit more willing. So I make sure I ask frequently. The more I ask, the more willing I become. Once the willingness becomes a reality, then there is usually very little effort involved in taking the next step.

～

When I got to this Step, I learned there is a big difference between Step Three and Step Six. In Step Three I make a decision. Do not get me wrong, this is a huge step. But after doing a complete moral inventory and then reading it to three of us God, sponsor, and myself—I found these next Steps were very wonderful and helped me to begin a growth of spirit I had no experience with. This was the beginning of the true relationship that I had made a decision to join.

The Sixth Step was where I actually can say I began a relationship with my Higher Power, whom I call God. Good relationships go two ways. What I can say is that when I really enter fully into this relationship, it is one I am proud of. At the beginning, God removed the desire to do drugs and alcohol. As our relationship grew, he removed my anxiety, depression, selfishness, and fear. He also removed my inability to do the things that held me back from accomplishing my goals. I was able to graduate from school and be of service to God in my work with people who are ill.

What I began to learn was that it is a give-and-take relationship. When I do things for other people or do things that God directs me to, I have God with me all the time. I never am alone. I now know how to speak to such an entity, asking that character defects ingrained in me, which I used to rely on, be removed.

I soon noticed people asking what was different about me. I was told I looked different and acted different. I shared what I did and what happened as a result. My eyes were wide open, clear, and inviting people in.

Step Six is built on the previous ones. The program is amazing how it builds on itself. There are Twelve Steps in a specific order, and I can now see they are this way for a purpose.

~

In Step Six, I need to become willing to have my Higher Power remove my character defects. I already turned my life and care over to my HP in Step Three and then shared my Fourth Step with Him. There were no more secrets. If I am fearful, I need to pray for the willingness to become willing to accomplish Step Six.

I started Step Six by reviewing my Fourth Step and was surprised to see so many shortcomings. In Step Four, I had identified feelings, thoughts, and actions that created havoc in my life, and now I was preparing to turn them over to God. I wasn't stuck with my flaws, and this gave me hope. My sponsor suggested that Step Six leads to removing the rough edges of my character, helping me become a more sincere, honest, and humble person.

The Sixth Step made me feel like I was an adult for the first time in my life. I was able to notice and take responsibility for fears, resentments, and negative reactions. Finally, I had words to describe what I thought and felt, such as impatient, judgmental, envious, demanding. This clarity empowered me to see my shortcomings when they appeared and to become willing to turn them over. The nearer I got to acknowledging and accepting the truth, the closer I got to freedom.

I used to get upset by people and events and didn't have any tools to deal with my frustrations. This stress made my pain and life worse. Now when I feel anything but love or serenity, I can return to my inventory and explore what is bothering me and how, in any given situation, I choose to see my part and be accountable. After naming the character defects that are troublesome, I become willing to let God remove them. Then I am ready for Step Seven.

Step Seven

Humbly asked Him to remove our shortcomings.

Ingredients

List of character defects (shortcomings)
Humility
Acceptance
Surrender of our agenda
God's will, not mine, be done
Prayer
Self-compassion
Daily practice
Faith and trust

Description

In this Step, we ask our Higher Power to remove what is in the way of our recovery progress. We desire a better life.

Directions

Humility means that we accept and love ourselves exactly as we are and realize we are not capable of healing ourselves with our attempts to control the situation. We need the assistance of a Power greater than ourselves. Supported by this acceptance, and trusting in the *care* of that Power we have been relying on since we *made a decision* in Step Three, we feel safe to be vulnerable and ask our Higher Power to remove our defects.

We don't give an agenda or a time frame for this removal to take place. That would be self-will. We take a leap of faith and place ourselves and our future into the care of our Higher Power.

We ask our Higher Power for help. We speak from the heart. We do this formally, so we know we've done it. Some people choose to do Step Seven by going to a special place in nature or somewhere that feels sacred, even if it's just a specific spot at home. It is a very personal moment between us and our Higher Power. We ask sincerely in our own way.

We don't dictate or request the terms or conditions by which our character defects are removed. Our Higher Power knows the timing and how and what to release. We let go and trust. If we don't have the willingness to let go, we pray for it.

Because it is natural to take our will back and not even notice we've done so, we have compassion for ourselves. We apply this Step daily. It can be useful to have a prayer that we say each day, so that we can recommit to our humility and invite our relationship with our Higher Power into the next twenty-four hours.

By humbly asking, daily, I am accepting what is my responsibility and what is the responsibility of my Higher Power. We are a team. My Higher Power is the pilot, and I am the copilot. I accepted that partnership, starting in Step Three. Now I utilize it every day, for the good of my life and the lives of all those around me. I am truly participating in the process of recovery.

Working the Step

1. What obstacles are there for me in this Step? What is needed to remove them?

2. Am I willing to put God's agenda ahead of my own?

3. What do I need to be willing to give my character defects to God?

4. What does humility look and feel like to me?

5. What shortcomings am I turning over?

6. Am I willing to be compassionate and forgiving toward myself as I work this Step?

7. What is most difficult to let go of?

8. How do I communicate with my Higher Power?

9. How will I ask my Higher Power to remove my shortcomings? What feels comfortable to me?

10. What ways can I incorporate Step Seven into a daily practice?

11. If I were to create my own daily Seventh-Step prayer to my Higher Power, what would I say?

What It Looks Like

I'd like to share an experience I had yesterday that showed me that a character defect I uncovered long ago, and which had been magnified by my chronic pain, can be removed, if only for the moment, by my Higher Power. I have always had a quick trigger when it comes to spilled milk, eggs dropped on the floor, the bottle of shampoo spilled in the shower, the dog throwing up on my carpet the day after it has been cleaned. My anger at those kinds of things has always been way out of proportion to the event itself.

As my chronic pain has worsened, so has my reaction to such events, especially if it means I am going to have to get down on the floor and clean up the mess. It hurts to get down there. My kids learned early on to disappear at such moments to avoid my wrath. And my poor hubby has, I am sure, cringed many times, when he has heard something in the kitchen hit the floor, followed by my voice uttering a stream of four-letter words.

So this is something I don't like about myself and that I have been working on for some time. And since joining CPA, I have known that the emotional overload that comes with it can clearly make my pain worse. When I first began working my Steps, I always wondered if practicing this Step actually worked. Would that particular defect really be removed by God?

Yesterday morning, at 6:00 a.m., my husband and I were getting dressed to go out. I was just getting out of the shower, when I heard his yelp, and looked out into the bedroom. There he stood, holding *the handle* of his coffee cup, which now lay, along with its contents, on my lovely, gold bedroom carpet.

A perfect setup for that quick-trigger reaction, right? Instead, with no effort at all, I told him to continue getting ready, and I reached for some towels to start mopping up. I didn't raise my voice. I didn't say anything I couldn't print in a family magazine. I didn't even think those thoughts.

This was not me! No way could this lady have pulled that off herself. I wasn't even reminding myself to stay cool. I was just calm and cool without trying. Now, can I rely on that little temper being gone forever? I don't think so, at least not yet. My experience has been that my defects leave slowly and can resurface if I don't continue to work the program. But for those of you who are doubting, as I did, it does work. And there is no doubt that not having built up a huge stress reaction by coming unglued meant my pain level was not increased for the day.

~

As I approach an upcoming trip, the fears of the unknown, the fears of being somewhere strange and in pain, the fears of having a body that is not predictable are looming large. All I can do, again and again, is pray to my Higher Power to remove these shortcomings. They are merely my tendency to go to the dark side and imagine the worst possible situations.

I pray for these shortcomings to be removed and then I take the action of returning to gratitude, many times a day. I remember to have gratitude for the love and support of my Higher Power who made this trip possible. I want to keep remembering that God will be with me every step of the way and that my fears are not a reflection of reality but *False Evidence Appearing Real*. The old habits of living in fear rather than living in faith are more obvious during times of change and stress. I humbly ask for help with this every day.

~

I don't think I'm unique in sometimes finding it easier to hang on to a defect rather than being willing to let it go. After all, I've lived with my defects all my life, and even though I don't like them, I'm comfortable with including them in who I am. To say I will give them up can be scary. Who will I be if I'm not arrogant? Will I be a timid mouse? And yet, I hate my arrogance as it pushes people away from me. They don't understand that it's a wall to protect myself.

I can get lost in this silly squirrel cage, going in circles as I try to find the humility to ask my Higher Power for help. And if I'm lucky, at some point I'll remember the little quote that hangs over my desk, which was given to me by my sponsor. It reads, *"If you let it go, it will stop screaming!"* How simple is that?

~

I have just gone through a bout of extra pain and am settling down now. I can tell that my foundations have been a bit shaken, as I am eating way more than usual. At times like this, I particularly like Step Seven because of the possibility of personal change. I know that I see the world in part through my character shortcomings. To let them go or have them removed suggests to me the possibility of having a brand new view or perception of the world.

Step Seven reminds me to pray. I cannot remove my shortcomings all by myself. I have to ask God. So often I think that I can do it myself. I must be willing to do my part, of course. I need to do the footwork and let go of the outcome. It's a joint effort, and that's a beautiful thing, yet it eludes me so often. It's like God is the surgeon, and I am the patient. If in Step Four I discovered a tumor, then in Step Six I have to do the footwork: get ready for, and be willing, to have the surgery. Then it is God's job, like the surgeon, to cut it out.

~

In Step Seven, we ask our Higher Power to help us get rid of the character defects that are present in us, sometimes even intensi-fied, because of our chronic pain and illness, and which prevent us from the peace and serenity we want in our lives. I found impa-tience, fearfulness, and laziness belonged on my list. If I'm finding myself being very impatient, I turn it over to my Higher Power. If I'm being fearful, I take the time to recommit myself to Step Two, when I came to believe in a Power greater than myself who could help me with these Steps. If I'm using my illness as an excuse for being lazy, I notice it and turn it over.

My *mouth* brings out the worst character defects in me. And the degree to which I use my sharp tongue to inflict hurt is di-rectly related to the level of my pain. On the days when my pain level is the highest, I am also the most arrogant, the most angry, the most negative, the most sarcastic. This insight gives me an opportunity to focus, on those days, and make an extra effort to be aware of this behavior and turn it over—to ask for help from my Higher Power.

~

In working Step Seven, I've found it useful to decide what the op-posite of a defect is. If I'm snappish because my pain level is high, I look for opportunities to say something nice to someone. One of my main defects is arrogance. I think no one understands my pain better than I do. So I look for opportunities to really empathize with someone who may be suffering, even if I don't think their pain is as "great" as mine. I "act as if" I do get it, and in so doing, I often find myself with a better attitude.

Step Eight

Made a list of all persons we had harmed, and became willing to make amends to them all.

Ingredients

Shift of focus

Trust in our foundation: Steps One to Seven

Review of Fourth Step inventory

Clarity about our part

Written list

Help from our sponsor

Prayer for willingness

Forgiveness

Honesty

Accountability

Discernment

Description

This is the first of the Twelve Steps in which we turn our focus to other people. In the first seven Steps, we have become aware of and accepted ourselves as we are: recognizing our powerlessness and insanity, discovering there is a Power greater than ourselves that is supporting us on our journey, looking fearlessly at all we have been and done, and sharing our inventory with another person. Then we have turned to our Higher Power with a clear list of attitudes and behaviors we want to let go of and asked God to remove them. We discovered our strengths and inner resources. We have a strong foundation now that we can trust—a clear, aware relationship with ourselves and with our Higher Power. But we do not live with ourselves and our Higher Power alone. We live in the world with people. Our foundation supports us now as we turn our focus outward and include those with whom we wish to live a life that is happy, joyous, and free.

It is not enough for us to understand and accept that we have behaved in ways that at best were ineffective and at worst led to anguish and suffering. The negative approaches we took to our circumstances took us down the wrong path. We have caused genuine harm—to ourselves and others. In this Step, we do two things: we take responsibility for the harm we have done and we become accountable by being willing to make amends. This necessary Step of putting the past behind us paves the way for us to do things differently from now on.

Directions

We begin by looking over our Step Four inventory to help us make a list of all the persons we have harmed.

When we live with chronic pain and illness, it may be that we need to put ourselves at the top of the list. Many of us have harmed ourselves as much, if not more, than anyone else. Putting our name at the top of the amends list, and with it the ways we have harmed ourselves, is a truly loving way to begin this Step. And it may make listing others and the harms we've caused them easier to acknowledge and put down in black and white.

We make a complete list of everyone we may have harmed and what the harm was. We focus on our behavior—what *we* did or said—not that of anyone else. It doesn't matter if they hurt us as well. We are focused on our side of the street only. Their side is not our concern. We accept responsibility for the consequences of past words and actions and become accountable for them by being willing to make amends. We omit no one, whether alive or not, whether we are still in contact or not. We look at our contribution to any difficult situation, listing all situations in which we have caused harm.

We don't concern ourselves with the type of amends we will make or what it will look like. That will be part of Step Nine. For now, our task is only to make the list and become willing. This gives us the freedom to really get clear about when, and to whom, we may have caused harm. We do not put ourselves under pressure to fix anything.

We make our list with discernment. To do that, we share our list with our sponsor. Left to our own devices, we may have a distorted sense of responsibility. We may feel like everything is our fault. Or we may feel that, in all situations, we were the victim. We may have caused harm to others and justified it. We look at the ways we have been cruel, negligent, and unkind to ourselves and others. We share the list with our sponsor so we are certain not to take either too much responsibility or too little.

This Step may take us time. We take it, as we do with all the Steps, in the spirit of love and compassion and guided by our Higher Power. The willingness involved may not come easily. We often find there are three categories of people and institutions on our list: those we are already willing to make amends to; those we might be able to make amends to someday; and those we feel we will never, ever be willing to make amends to. We pray about it and go forward at our own pace. As we do so, we find ourselves changing, however slowly or quickly. The day comes when we are surprised to find that those in the "never" category have made their way onto our willing-to list. How is this possible?

Forgiveness is crucial. We forgive others, and we forgive ourselves, so we can be set free. Holding on to resentments, anger, and hate keeps us bound to the past and to pain. Taking this Step makes it possible to stop our fixation on the past and hanging on to it. It is the key to letting go. We want to be freed of the weights that keep us tied to the past and reliving old wounds and hurts. By taking responsibility for our part, we can be freed from pain in ways we thought were not possible.

Working the Step

1. Am I willing to list all those I have harmed, and how I harmed them, without exception? If not, am I willing to pray for the willingness to do so?

2. Have I put myself on my amends list? If not, why not?

3. Have I asked my sponsor for help identifying where I may have harmed others?

4. What blocks me from being willing to make amends?

5. Are there people or institutions on my list that I feel completely unwilling to make amends to? If so, am I willing to name them and pray for the willingness?

6. How has Step Eight helped me take responsibility for my actions and words?

7. How has this Step helped me break free from resentments?

8. Did I use my Fourth Step inventory to guide me? How did it help me?

9. Do I understand the difference between being willing and making the amends?

10. How does my Higher Power help me with this Step?

11. Did I notice any patterns in doing this Step? What did I learn about myself?

12. What benefits do I experience in working Step Eight?

What It Looks Like

When I heard that I might have to make amends to someone I may have harmed because I, *me*, live with chronic pain and illness . . . well, I just couldn't relate to that. Hadn't other people caused me harm by the way they treated me because of my chronic illness? Hadn't other people hurt me by leaving me out of gatherings, parties, and so on because they felt I couldn't make it or handle it?

However, I did learn, in Steps One, Two, and Three, that despite my chronic pain and illness, I had been selfish at times, that I had hurt other people and in some cases turned them out of my life. I also learned in Steps Four and Five that I had some character defects, some "negative coping mechanisms," as one of my CPA friends puts it. I found out some things about myself that I didn't necessarily like and which I wanted to change. It is from my work on Step Four that I can begin to make the list of people I may have harmed.

Step Eight is just about making the list. Making the actual amends takes place in the Ninth Step. This has definitely been a sponsor-guided Step, for me. It is after I make my list that I become *willing* to make amends. I acquire the quality of willingness.

~

There are obvious names that should go on my Eighth-Step list. There are also names I'm not too sure about, and this is where my sponsor can help. And then there are a few names of people who have wronged me so significantly that I feel they don't deserve an amends for wrongs done to them. Getting past this and making sure all the people I've harmed are on my list was done by making a list with three columns.

The first column is titled "make amends as soon as possible." This is a list of those obvious names. The second column is titled "make amends when appropriate." This is the list of people where I might need my sponsor's help to determine if an amends is truly needed. And finally, the third column is titled "I won't ever make amends to these people; they hurt me far more than I hurt them." It wasn't till I realized that it was OK to have some names in that third column that I was able to see more clearly where I had caused harm to another.

Over time, as I did my Ninth Step, I made amends to the people in the first column and found that some names from the second column moved over to the first. There were also instances where my sponsor suggested I owe no amends or may owe one, but to do it directly would cause more harm than good. And while working on the first two columns, I found, much to my surprise, that some of the names in the third column moved all the way over to the first column, and I became willing to make those amends.

Completing Steps Eight and Nine can be a slow but extremely rewarding process, most especially when those tough amends in the third column have been made. There were some amends for which I waited to receive my HP's guidance for the appropriate time and place. The willingness to make them will come if we ask for it, but it may take a while. It took me several years to find the willingness to make all the amends needed. The result of getting to that point brought a wonderful freedom in knowing I have swept clean "my side of the street."

～

I was surprised when my sponsor reminded me to put myself on the list. I knew that when I was in pain I was often not nice to my family members, but I hadn't even considered that I was not nice to myself either. This was a revelation. One behavior I became aware of was the voice that jabbered in my head. I would speak to myself in a cruel way that I would never say out loud to anyone in my life.

～

Some questions that I asked myself to help decide who should go on my Step Eight list:

1. Who has been the recipient of my anger as a result of this pain and illness?
2. Who have I laid a "guilt trip" on, giving them the "poor me" attitude so I can get more attention?
3. Who have I outright lied to about my pain and illness, making it seem worse than it is so I won't have to do something difficult?
4. Who have I made a promise to about doing something that I knew up front was going to be too much for me?

~

I made my Step Eight list from my Fourth Step inventory. This Step is not about making amends, just making a list. Taking inventory in Step Four gave me a lot of information to use as I looked it over and began to see my part. The amends is not about what people did to me, or what I thought they did, but about looking at how I have hurt others and about clearing up my side of the street.

~

The first part of Step Eight says, "made a list of persons we had harmed." So that's just it, make a list. The actual doing of the amends will take place in Step Nine. And the second part of Step Eight says, "became willing to make amends to them all." So to me, that part asks me "to become willing." I often have to pray for the willingness in many aspects of my recovery. Since I can complicate things so much, it was helpful for me to think of Step Eight in two simple parts: making a list and becoming willing to make amends.

Step Nine

Made direct amends to such people,
wherever possible, except when to do so
would injure them or others.

Ingredients

Prayer for guidance and willingness
Courage
Consultation with sponsor
Right timing
Changed attitude and behavior
Patience
Prudence
Humility
Love
No attachment to outcome (NATO)/no expectations

Description

This is a cleansing Step. In Step Nine, we demonstrate with our speech and actions that we have changed, and we choose to be of benefit to ourselves and others. We clear up the past and attempt to repair what was damaged. As we do so, we are making steps toward a different future. Choosing new actions will result in new and different outcomes. In doing Step Nine, we stop being an enemy to ourselves and become a friend. It is an empowering and life-changing Step.

Directions

There is a difference between an amends and an apology. An apology says "I'm sorry" for the trouble or harm caused and stops there. It does not include a commitment to change, to not repeat the behavior. Though often we do apologize in Step Nine, we do not stop with that. We admit our errors, and we correct them. We have the willingness to do things differently.

We are honest and fair and mature. We have made mistakes, and now we don't increase the pain we've caused by beating ourselves up. We find relief in this Step. We release ourselves from the guilt and shame we've been holding onto.

We are seeking peace of mind, as this is what it will take for us to move forward. In making amends, we learn that we *can* clean up the past. We may have thought we were the victims, but since we have looked deeply, we've seen how our attitudes, words, and actions caused suffering, for ourselves and others. We can change our attitudes and behaviors. By making amends, we set ourselves free.

With simplicity, we take responsibility. We state our errors and our role in the harm caused. Then we commit to not repeating our behavior in the future. We ask how we can right the harm we caused. Making amends is taking action. We don't just apologize, we change.

This takes courage. Of course we may have fear—being accountable for harms we have caused is not usually considered fun or easy. But courage is not the absence of fear, it is facing the task ahead, fearful or not, and walking through it. It may not be easy, but it needs to be done. With courage, we find we are able to take the actions required.

Amends are "esteemable acts," and they result in a reliable new level of self-esteem.

Step Nine is a humbling Step. We need to be tactful and considerate of others when we make our amends. We make restitution more through our deeds than our words. And when we do, we find our lives change for the better—almost immediately.

What might amends look like? Sometimes they are done directly, face to face. As the Step states, we make a considerable effort to do them in this way if it will not cause further harm. But sometimes direct amends are not possible. We ask our Higher Power for guidance and consult with our sponsor so we can identify the most appropriate amends to make in each circumstance. We ask the question, "What do I need to do to repair the situation?" Then we take the necessary actions to bring about reparation.

It is essential that we ask for help. Because we are taking on new behavior, we cannot rely on our past experiences to guide us. So we set out with good companions at our side. We rely on the strength we receive from our Higher Power and our friends in the fellowship. Our sponsor and our Higher Power help us discern what is appropriate to do and say and when, so that we don't cause further harm. With each and every amends, we have faith we will be guided to take the next right action at the right time.

In some cases, we may not be able to reach the person we owe an amends to or honestly feel bewildered about the best way to go about it. As always, we ask our Higher Power for direction and discuss the options with our sponsor. If someone has died, we may choose someone else who would benefit from our new behavior to make our amends to in their stead. Or we may visit their gravesite and simply speak or read a letter to them. If someone is still alive but we're not sure if getting in touch with them directly would cause more harm, we can write a letter and share it with our sponsor or a trustworthy friend. We do this before and/or instead of sending it.

When it comes to amends to ourselves, writing a letter to ourselves and sharing it with our sponsor, laying out what we intend to do differently from now on, can be very effective. In this process, we get to experience what it is like to have someone lovingly make amends to us, and we are empowered more fully to go forward with others on our list.

By choosing new behaviors in old situations, we make *living* amends. We are already doing this by being in this program and working these Steps, but in Step Nine, we do it consciously with others in mind. We do it with consideration, purpose, commitment, and action.

It is important, in fact vital, that we not make amends hoping for a specific outcome. We take Step Nine to clean *our* house, to make up for *our* mistakes, and to free ourselves of long-held guilt and shame. We cannot afford to focus on hoped-for or expected outcomes, as such a focus would only indicate we are still self-seeking, which would be repeating old behavior. Without an expectation for a particular response, if we *Keep It Simple* and stay on our side of the street, we will truly be behaving differently and offering ourselves into a life that is of benefit to all beings. We will discover and receive gifts we could not have imagined, instead of only the ones we may have thought of and wished for. We are inviting our Higher Power into our lives in a very real way when we take Step Nine, and changes of great value may come our way. This is only possible if we let go of the outcomes and remain open to what unfolds.

This Step will be started today, but it may take some time to complete fully. It is the beginning of the process of cleaning up our side of the street. It may not be done perfectly, but we do it sincerely. And we don't do it alone. We are following our Higher Power's will, not our own. We get to choose the kind of person we want to be today and the kinds of relationships we want in our lives. We make those choices, take action, and let go.

By making amends, we put into active practice our new commitment to live confident, happy lives that are free of resentments, guilt, and shame. We offer ourselves to our Higher Power and ask for guidance in how to truly move forward in new ways in our spiritual development.

According to the "Big Book" of Alcoholics Anonymous, it is by working this Step that we discover "a new freedom and a new happiness." Those who have walked this path ahead of us attest to the truth of this assertion.

Working the Step

1. Is there anything in the way of my willingness to do this Step? If so, what is needed so I can progress?

2. In what ways did I apply honesty and humility in this Step?

3. How does making amends help me build balanced and healthy relationships?

4. How did I manage the anxiety that arose while working this Step?

5. Did I turn to my sponsor and Higher Power in working this Step?

6. In what ways did I repair and not just apologize for the harm I caused?

7. Have I made amends to myself? How?

8. Did making amends to myself have any effect on my amends to others? In what way?

9. What stops me from making direct amends?

10. What are my motives in making amends?

11. Did I ask my sponsor for help to understand which amends might create further harm?

12. How will I make amends in the situations in which I can't make direct amends?

13. How were the slogans *Easy Does It* and *Keep It Simple* useful to me in this Step?

What It Looks Like

My sponsor told me that in Step Nine I first needed to ask my Higher Power for help. My connection to my Higher Power, whom I call God, had deepened over the last months, and I was now ready to take on Step Nine, the last of the action Steps. In Steps Four through Eight, I had brought all my past to light. In this Step, I was able to clear out everything inside of myself that was holding me back. I needed to be willing, and then I needed to let go of how I thought this should be done. This Step happens on God's timing, not mine. I began releasing all that kept me suffering emotionally, and it was an immense release. I felt liberation from all my yester-years and discovered a new freedom.

~

Some amends sit on my list for years. I wait patiently for God to bring the right timing and situation into my life. Then it just flows. It has been eight years since one person was first put onto my list. This past week, an opportunity presented itself in which I could simply and easily say the few words that needed to be said. It was not a big production, which it would have been years ago. It did not recreate pain for either of us. It was well received and appreciated and I felt liberated.

~

I am very lucky to have a husband who enjoys just having me by his side in our home. I have a tendency to sit in the chair that causes me the least pain and another tendency to go to bed when I feel the time is best for me. I have considerable problems sleeping, and I find that the timing of going to bed is a factor, as well as the supplements and drugs that I use to give me a restful night's sleep. Both of these things leave my husband feeling hurt and unloved.

This isn't about sex; it's about being physically close. It is important to his well-being in our relationship that we have time when we are just next to each other—sitting next to each other on the couch or snuggling under the covers at bedtime. This is something I have to consciously work on. I can make amends to my husband by not always going to the chair that is comfortable for me but sometimes heading to the couch to sit at his side and sometimes going to bed before I feel that I can sleep, just to be with him and make him feel loved. Both of these things are something of a compromise for me, but they are minimal sacrifices, especially compared to the results. This is one way I am learning to make amends to my husband.

~

The most important amends I've had to make in CPA is to my wonderful husband. At the time we met, I was still the Energizer Bunny. He often referred to my "steel-trap mind." My biggest fear when I decided to move in with him was that he wouldn't be able to keep up with me. I had a few unexplained pains at that point but just blamed them on getting older. Within a year of moving in with him, my disease exploded in all its ugly "glory!" Fatigue and pain became constant companions. The brain fog that is part of my illness resulted in him teasingly calling me "flea brain." The steel-trap mind was gone.

The worst part was my anger—at the pain, at the doctors who couldn't fix it, at God for dumping this on me when I had finally found my soulmate. The recipient of all that anger was my husband. He hadn't bargained for this, and I found myself actually starting arguments, hoping he would end the relationship, because I certainly didn't deserve his love. I was "damaged goods." It took me a good three years to realize that he wasn't going to walk away, and I was finally able to make the amends I needed to make.

I'd love to say that ended my bad behavior, but I still find myself making amends for snapping at him or greeting his idea to do something fun with no enthusiasm. But I'm getting better at it. Step Nine in this case leads me right into Step Ten, where I daily reflect to be sure I haven't crossed that line again. And when I do, he often responds with "that's the pain talking, isn't it?" I am so blessed to have found this program that literally saved my relationship.

~

I got really stuck on my Ninth Step when I tried it the first time. Some amends were really easy to make. Others, not so much! Finally someone offered his approach, and it worked for me. He said he had put all his amends on a piece of paper with three columns. The first column was for the amends he would make right away—the easy ones. The second column was for the amends he would make when the opportunity presented itself. And the third column was for the amends he was convinced he would never be able to make.

Well, I tried his method and found out exactly what he had. By the time I finished doing the ones in the first column, some of those in the second column had moved over, and I was able to make them right away. And that continued to happen. And that third column? The ones I thought I could never face? The ones too scary to contemplate? Somehow, without my interference or even permission, those amends eventually moved across the board to the first column and I was able to make them.

Today, there are no names in any columns. I keep those columns clean by making amends immediately after something occurs. I just don't let those resentments build up. That's what the Tenth Step is all about.

~

Step Nine means staying open-minded to my HP so that I can be as open/honest and aware as possible about the role of chronic illness and pain in my life and how I have managed and mostly mismanaged my condition and symptoms by thinking that I could control them. And so Step Nine is practicing being compassionate with myself, especially as I learn how to find balance between overdoing and underdoing. Instead of corrosive self-castigation,

I'm able to stop and be in a living amends with my HP, myself, and my present situation.

This past Sunday was my son's birthday. Taking him and his family out to dinner was something I wanted to do (and did do), but I made all kinds of wrong decisions about what I could accomplish during the day. I did set aside two hours to rest and get ready before going out, but I had tried to do too much earlier in the day and was agitated, in pain, and tense. I made amends to myself and my family by consciously, verbally—out loud to myself—surrendering all the negative feelings and thoughts to my HP before I left. We had an enjoyable time together.

∼

Step Nine is not a to-do list of tasks. It requires willingness and patience. There are many ways I've worked this Step in CPA.

One way I make amends is simply to begin behaving in new ways. I needed to make amends to my friends for all the times I said, "I'm fine," and then behaved irritably and unpleasantly because I was really feeling miserable. So the next time I was in pain and out with my friends, I made amends by doing it differently. I told them, "I am in pain today. I want to be here with you, but I am not feeling great. I may be quiet today, and that is OK."

Some of my amends were to people no longer in my life. So in the new relationships in my life, I made amends to the people from my past. I became aware in Step Four of the ways I treated certain people poorly during difficult bouts of illness. Today, when I encounter similar situations with someone new in my life, I conduct myself differently. For me, like all Step work, these amends are not meant to cause more pain. I do it to deepen my spiritual recovery and take responsibility for my actions. It is done in partnership with my HP and supported by my sponsor and the fellowship.

Step Ten

*Continued to take personal inventory and when
we were wrong promptly admitted it.*

Ingredients

Awareness and self-examination
Kindness and self-compassion
Accountability
Behavior change
Daily practice
Commitment
Choosing well-being over suffering
Trust in Higher Power

Description

Recovery is an ongoing process. By continuing to apply the Steps to each day, we find ourselves leading happy, fulfilled, meaningful lives. We have shifted our focus from being self-guided to Spirit-guided—the work of a lifetime. Now we continue on that journey. In Step Ten, we make a commitment to keep going.

In Steps One, Two, and Three, we made decisions that put us on a spiritual path. In Steps Four through Nine, we took the actions necessary to remove all that keeps us separated from our Higher Power and from living in harmony with our fellow human beings. In Step Ten, we maintain our spiritual fitness by staying focused on the Steps and deepening our application of them over time. One day at a time, one moment at a time, we choose to continue to take our inventory, to make amends when we have caused harm, and to be of service.

Directions

We are human, and we will make mistakes. It is not a question of *if* but *when* we will err in our judgment, our words, or our actions. But now we have a program, and we have tools to help us face whatever comes our way. In Step Ten, we use those tools. If we cause harm, we no longer need to live with the shame and guilt, the burdens of our errors. We can repair what is broken. We stay aware and are accountable. And where we are powerless to make changes, we turn things over to our Higher Power, trusting that "God is doing for us what we cannot do for ourselves."

Daily, and throughout the day, we examine our behavior and take responsibility for it. When we are wrong, we promptly correct it. We repair right away.

Metaphorically speaking, if we discover we've left the faucet running and we go back to shut off the tap as soon as we see we've made this mistake, we will not cause a flood. It may make a mess, but we clean that up and hope it's a small one. Similarly, we strive in Step Ten to keep our messes manageable, knowing we are human and are bound to make mistakes now and then. We have compassion for ourselves *and* we are accountable. This sets us free to live as we are—imperfect and honest.

And should our messes be complicated, we now have a relationship with a Power greater than ourselves. We turn to our Higher Power and ask for help, for guidance, for strength. If we notice we continually or habitually act in ways that are harmful, perhaps discovering a defect of character that was hidden before, we ask our Higher Power to remove our negative ways. This is how we "live in the solution."

We are watching for when we are selfish, dishonest, resentful, and fearful. We notice which defects of character have come into play, and we ask for these to be removed. We call our sponsor or another program member, consider the most appropriate action, or whether one is needed, and commit to making amends as soon as possible. We shift our thinking toward being of service to others. Our focus moves away from self-centeredness, and we help someone else. This is how the obsession with our pain and illness, all the problems of our bodies and minds, will be lessened.

We don't fight people. We don't fight our bodies. We don't fight systems. A miracle occurs, and we no longer try to battle and control our symptoms. We also don't ignore them. We are in a position of neutrality, of acceptance and awareness. We are neither arrogant nor afraid. We do our part and only our part. We let our Higher Power handle the rest.

This brings us a truly new sense of serenity, and we find we want to maintain it. We monitor our actions and attitudes through ongoing self-examination. This is a continuous effort in our recovery. We make an intention in the morning to be of service to our Higher Power and others, and we do spot checks throughout the day. How are we doing? At the end of the day, we assess and review the past twenty-four hours. We look at what we did well, what we are grateful for, and what we did less well than we would have wanted. We look at where fear, resentment, dishonesty, and selfishness have appeared. We ask our Higher Power to remove any negative patterns.

We discuss anything that gnaws at us, such as where we feel we may owe an amends, with our sponsor or another program friend, and we make amends if we have harmed anyone, including ourselves. We take all these actions promptly, as soon as we become aware of how we have caused harm.

Step Ten may seem like a process of continual self-reproach, but in practice, it is exactly the opposite. Spiritual growth requires us to be honest about what we do and who we are. Making an amends means that we don't keep repeating the same behavior. By developing a daily habit of self-awareness, making sure we include gratitude and recognition of where we have done well, as well as the places where we wish we'd done better, we are set free of recrimination, self-doubt, and worry. This reduces our stress on all levels. It is a continual process of course correction.

We come to understand a very relieving concept: our suffering, and our freedom, is always within us, even though we may want to blame others. When we see areas in which we have created our own pain—emotional, physical, mental—and correct it, it becomes easy to choose happiness as a way of life. Working Step Ten, we get to do this every day.

We have started out on a lifelong process of spiritual renewal and growth. Step Ten is a daily commitment to continue maturing in wisdom. We acknowledge when we have erred and we make adjustments. We are just like others. We are not perfect. We practice sincere honesty and great compassion. We are all doing our very best, and we will fail to realize our goals at times. In recovery, we call it a "slip" when we fall back into old behaviors. Slips are part of being human. When we have one, we admit it and make amends as needed.

As we strengthen the resilience of our minds and hearts, we can cope with whatever happens to our bodies.

Working the Step

1. How does this Step improve my emotional balance and well-being?

2. How does this Step help me be aware of ways I harm myself and others?

3. What does it mean to "promptly admit it"?

4. What is leading to my resistance to working Step Ten? Have I looked at ways to remove the blocks and asked my Higher Power for help?

5. How has Step Ten supported my sanity? My happiness?

6. How have I recognized that a complete amends means a commitment to change and to avoid repeating the same behaviors?

7. In what ways do I see self-will operating in my life?

8. Am I committed to ongoing spiritual development?

9. How do I incorporate this Step into each day?

10. Do I make note of my good qualities in my daily inventory, as well as those that cause harm?

11. What is the value of a spot-check inventory? How do I use this tool?

What It Looks Like

Once I completed the Steps leading up to this one, I found that I had cleared up a lot of wreckage from the past. But that wasn't sufficient, because I am human and I make lots of mistakes. So the way to stay current with my program is to work Step Ten. It is how I continue to keep my side of the street clean. To me, Step Ten is a daily, even hourly, opportunity to be human, to err, and to make adjustments as I go along. It reminds me that I am a work in progress. So when I make a wrong choice, there is room to start over and make a new choice and grow as a person. This has been one of the most used tools in my Twelve-Step kit over the years.

~

I have pain and I get easily tired, and that is often when my ability to cope with the everyday challenges of life becomes compromised. When my symptoms are frequent and intense, the tasks that normally are no big deal seem overwhelming and impossible. This is usually when the tone of my voice gets sharper and my impatience shows up. My emotions seem to take over my mouth, and words come out that I regret.

I am accountable for my words and actions, even when I feel poorly. Step Ten makes it possible for me to repair my mistakes so I can move forward with love and respect for myself and others. It is a Step that brings me back to where I started in Step One: humility.

~

Generally, when I make a mistake, I have an immediate gut reaction that tells me something is not right. With Step Ten, I can clear the slate if something is bothering me. I might wait to act on it, as I may have to talk to someone else first to know what amends to make. When I take things personally, I might react in ways I regret. Do I need verbal amends or to change my behavior? It helps to explore with someone else and determine what is necessary.

~

I love this Step because it is about keeping the focus on myself and not about other people's inventory. It is about me feeling comfortable in my own skin. I'm the only one who can and needs to change, and often it is about my attitude. I have to ask for help from my Higher Power. It also helps to share the situation with another person to get clarity.

~

One thing that I learned from my sponsor in CPA is the importance of paying attention to my behaviors, my feelings, my traits—all of me. The way I look at this spot-check inventory is that I am taking stock regularly. Having an objective view of myself, and deciding the qualities I want to keep and those I want to ask my Higher Power to remove, is changing me in positive ways.

Even though I don't formally write out this Step Ten inventory, with the new awareness it brings throughout the day, I am willing to promptly admit when I'm wrong and to make amends, not just apologize. The point is, I'm willing to grow along spiritual lines.

~

My husband was angry with me yesterday. He said, "No matter what I do, nothing is good enough for you." For the last few days, I had been in a bad mood, in pain, quite tired and irritable, and unpleasant to live with. I was feeling self-pity, falsely believing "poor me" had to put up with an incompetent husband because he didn't do what I needed when I needed it and how I needed it. I had to stop and apologize. I was in the wrong. It was not about him. He didn't do anything wrong. He was being kind and going out of his way to help me. I used my illness as an excuse for my negative behavior, and I had to make amends.

~

When I am in pain and worn out emotionally and physically, I find that I can "act out" and blame others during my day for not treating me the way I want to be treated. And that's where I see the Tenth Step coming into play in my life. I can become short-tempered when I am worn down, and so I need to take extra care of myself at those times so I won't "act out" and curse the bus driver or anyone else along my way.

~

There are a few tools I can use to help me with Step Ten. The first of these is the "spot-check inventory." Throughout the day, I use this tool to "check" on my behavior and quickly catch times when I have fallen back into old habits and feelings. I use this tool any time I am feeling "uncomfortable" with a situation, or conversation, or my own reaction to either of these. It is usually pretty easy to see when I'm in the wrong, and admitting it right then and there takes much of the angst out of the amends process.

The second tool is a "daily inventory." This works best for me in the evening, when I can do a self-check to see if that feeling of discomfort with my own behavior is still there. Perhaps I didn't take the time to make an amends on the spot. Or perhaps it is only in reflection that I see something I missed at the time . . . something I said or did that may have hurt someone else.

Finally, there is the "long-term inventory." This is similar to the Fourth Step inventory, except that I focus on current feelings and behaviors rather than returning to the past. I do this at least once a year, sometimes several times. I find it is best to work with my sponsor when performing this inventory.

~

By continuing to take a personal inventory and promptly addressing my miscues, I can leave each day behind knowing I haven't created any further baggage. I am free of the guilt, remorse, and anger that once dominated my life. My sponsor reminds me that I will continue to have little slips in behavior or thinking along the way. Step Ten helps me catch myself before I slip any further. After years of practice, it has become a way of life, and it has added an ingredient of integrity and self-respect that my life had been missing for a long time.

~

When I was first confronted by something my son said, I was taken back and quite angry. "How could you possibly say this about me?" was my initial thought and prepared response. Luckily I didn't go there. I stopped and thought for a moment. I didn't let my old "victim self" kick in. In a calm voice I asked, "I hear your anger with me. What brought that about?" The calm voice was key.

He replied, "Dad, just five minutes ago you did something you wanted to do. Now I ask for something I need and you can't do it because you are in pain. Did it come about that quickly? I think you're just using it as an excuse." He then walked out of the room.

I had been in pain all afternoon. Yet I was able to do what I wanted, and I did it in spite of the pain. When my son made a relatively simple request, I did opt out because of my pain. He was right. Step Ten was in order! I was wrong and had to make amends right then.

Step Eleven

Sought through prayer and meditation to improve our conscious contact with God as we understood Him, praying only for knowledge of His will for us and the power to carry that out.

Ingredients

Prayer
Meditation practice
Daily commitment
Daily renewal of contact with Higher Power
Thy will be done—putting our Higher Power's will above our own
Faith
Wisdom
Spiritual strength

Description

This is the Step where we deepen and strengthen our relationship
with a Power greater than ourselves. By daily practice of meditation
and prayer, oriented toward our personal Higher Power, we
develop "conscious contact." We are now in a relationship with
the God of our understanding that is intimate and that supports
us in being our best selves, living lives with more fullness and
well-being than we could have previously imagined.

It is said that prayer is talking to God, and meditation is
listening. We listen in order to receive guidance. Both of these
practices put us in direct contact with our Higher Power.

Directions

We need daily quiet time. Some of us take time in the morning—
we may get on our knees, first thing, and ask to have our defects
removed for one more day. We may sit in meditation for ten
minutes, or thirty, or whatever amount of time works for us. We
may write to the God of our understanding in our journal or take
time-outs during the day to check in with our Higher Power and
seek His will in whatever current circumstance we are facing.

We ask our Higher Power to direct us and bring that direction
into our motivation for the day. We recall or establish our

intention. We ask to be aware and accepting. We ask for the power to carry out our Higher Power's will for us, whatever that may be. We notice when we don't want what we have and when we want what we don't have. We see how that is only a continuation of being run by self-will, of not accepting "what is" with gratitude.

At any time during the day we can *pause* to pray or meditate, or both. We notice and ask ourselves, are we focused again on our own will? We can stop and ask God for direction, listen for guidance, and take the next indicated action.

Prayer and meditation may be unfamiliar to us. We likely need to set aside some time each day to practice our interpretation of these. If we begin to practice them, they will become powerful supports in our daily life. We will find a stability of mind and calmness of spirit.

There are many ways to meditate and pray. We experiment with what works best for us and know that, just like our relationship with our Higher Power, our methods will evolve over time. We may start the day asking God for inspiration, for guidance, for help with our actions and words. We may read something inspirational, using that as part of our daily meditation and prayer. We can ask to be shown the next indicated action throughout the day. We ask to be freed from self-will and to think of others and be willing to be of service on this day. We pause throughout the day and ask for guidance. We ask that "Thy will be done" when we are lost or confused, in doubt, or caught up in intense emotions. In the evening, we review our day and our choices and pray for guidance for what we can do differently in our ongoing efforts toward serenity, contentment, and peace.

In this Step, we stop *using* God: "Oh please, God, make my pain and illness go away!" Instead, we ask God to use us: "Please, God, show me how I can be of service today." Eleventh Step prayer is not telling our Higher Power what we want. It is asking what our Higher Power wants and aligning ourselves with that. We ask how we can serve, as well as how we can have meaning in our lives by serving our Higher Power's purposes. We ask for strength to deal with the problems before us. Our Higher Power can guide us, based on the qualities of patience, love, compassion, kindness, and acceptance. When we seek this guidance, we find new direction and confidence.

We need to be humble enough and quiet enough to receive God's help. Sometimes our Higher Power speaks through an intuitive thought, a new clarity, or an inspiration. Other times, our answers come from something we hear at a meeting or read in our literature. We can trust the guidance we receive when it is based in honesty, genuine love and kindness, and unselfishness. To find wisdom beyond our own capacity requires *contact* with our Higher Power, which is made through prayer and meditation.

We work this Step daily, not once in a while and not just when we are in great pain, having intense symptoms, or are in crisis. This way, just as we would if we were going to a gym, we develop our spiritual muscles and increase our capacity for wisdom, serenity, and happiness. We deepen and improve our conscious contact. It may take some effort to pray and meditate, but the fruits are worth it.

Any relationship we truly care about takes time and attention. What is exciting and wonderful about the relationship we are creating with our Higher Power is that we find that whenever we reach out, our Higher Power is there. And if there is ever a moment when we do not feel met or responded to by God, we discover that God reveals more to us in time. Our relationship with our Higher Power will likely become one of the most intimate and effectively supportive relationships of our lives.

Many who have worked this program before us have found miraculous solutions to problems they thought unsolvable by simply letting go of their own will and listening for God's. By hearing of others working this Step, at meetings and in conversation, we learn that we each have our own Higher Power, in whose care we have put our will and our lives (Step Three). We discover that our Higher Power has far more love for us than we could have possibly imagined. The solutions we find when we follow our Higher Power's guidance are often unexpected and would not have otherwise occurred to us if we did not take the time to pray (ask) and listen (meditate).

When we do this, we will see a change. We will find calm, faith, happiness, and wisdom.

Working the Step

1. How do I make conscious contact with my Higher Power?

2. What does my meditation practice look like?

3. How do I understand prayer?

4. What is my plan to put this Step into action on a daily basis?

5. How am I going to open myself up to God's will?

6. How do I benefit from conscious contact with my Higher Power?

7. How do I understand "Thy will, not mine, be done"?

8. How do I know what is God's will?

9. What is blocking me from doing this Step today? Am I willing to pray for these blocks to be removed?

10. In what ways have I seen "more being revealed over time"?

11. Am I willing to commit daily to my spiritual recovery?

12. How does this Step support me throughout the day?

13. How would I describe my relationship with my Higher Power as it is today?

14. How do I experience "the power to carry that out"?

What It Looks Like

Prayer and meditation take practice. It helps me to listen and learn about how other people establish their important conscious contact. For me, meditation is the most challenging to practice. How can I quiet my mind when my body is screaming at me? One little minute at a time, that's how! Depending on the day, meditation or prayer may work better. I've learned that what is most important is to just do it.

~

Prayer is something I already love and is a fairly regular part of my daily life. Meditation is something I do on and off but would like to do more. Many years of my life were spent doing my own thing and hoping it was God's will because, by golly, I was going to do what I wanted. I wanted God's will, but not enough to change my path if I really wanted something else more. These days I now want God's will most of the time—more than I want my will. That is an improvement.

~

When my chronic pain and illness are acting up, it is a blessed relief to turn it over to God and see how I can spend my time well, instead of giving in to depression and self-pity and fear. When I see days lost because I'm not feeling well and can't "do anything," it can help if I take time to pray, meditate, and come to peace and acceptance for the circumstances I am in now.

Can I trust God in this chronic situation? Am I willing to? By seeking to improve my conscious contact with God, I am taking a step toward a day that has at least some acceptance and therefore a possibility of accomplishing something: sinking into needed rest instead of fretting; maybe time spent quietly doing things that enrich my life, even if they are not the things I originally had planned for the day; peacefulness.

~

Step Eleven is something I can practice every moment of every day. When I'm not thinking about something that happened yesterday or busy with thoughts of tomorrow, I am free to focus on right now. One day at a time, I work to stay mindful of the moment. When I can do this, I am open to receive the messages God sends. I am aware of the words that come through my loved ones, my friends, and even perfect strangers. Messages come through the voice of my sponsor and others in recovery, through the music I listen to, and the books that I read.

And the messages don't always come in the form of words. They can be delivered by way of a loving hug from a child or a smile from a stranger at just the right time. They can come in a dream or a series of coincidences. I can't always meditate, but I can be conscious in the moment and ask what can be learned.

Experience has taught me to pay attention when the same message seems to come from many different sources. When I'm attentive to the moment, the messages are constant, clear, and undeniable.

~

It was hard to find the time in the morning for prayer and meditation, as I am not a morning person. And I was trying to get to work while sick with pain and illness. One day, I decided I would not get up but would just lie in bed and pray. I discovered I had to determine each day, how am I feeling? Is this a day to stay in bed or go to work? I needed guidance from my Higher Power every day. It was

like my day wasn't good if I didn't have that time to pray and meditate. My prayer was "Please help me; I am in pain. Will I get up and
try to get to work today?" Starting my morning this way gave me
the foundation to begin each day with clarity and strength.

~

This Step has given me more peace and contentment and acceptance of my physical condition and the limitations I have as a result. I incorporate gratitude with this Step. Making a gratitude list
two or three times a day is a form of prayer for me. Throughout
the day, I just say "thank you" for whatever is presented this moment, even when I am in pain. I say to God, "I don't like this; I don't
know why this is happening in my life, but it is here." I will trust a
gift will come from this and say "thank you" to my Higher Power.
This changes my energy and helps a lot.

~

I've always been able to pray. Meditation has been my stumbling
block. If prayer is said to be me talking to God and meditation is
God talking to me, then I'm missing out on the best part, because
my head never shuts up long enough for God to get a word in
edgewise. Lately, I've been practicing meditation to quiet my mind
so I can hear my Higher Power and using prayer to calm my soul
and talk to my Higher Power.

~

My brain has been on fast-forward all my life. Even my prayers are
short. And when I try to sit quietly and meditate, the clamoring
in my head drowns out most everything else. I used to feel "less
than" because I never seemed to be able to quiet my mind.

Through working the Steps in recovery, I have discovered a few things. God doesn't hold it against me that the committee in my head doesn't shut up long enough for me to hear him. He uses others to send me the message that he wants me to hear: in face-to-face meetings; in one-on-one conversations, with sponsors and others who have a spiritual life that I admire. He knows I'm trying, and he hasn't abandoned me.

∿

It is important for me to practice prayer and meditation daily. I am comfortable in the silence and look forward to resting into it. At these times, I have a strong feeling of serenity. When the serenity is absent, I pray for help. This is good practice for when I am in the middle of a challenging situation. In that moment, I can become aware of my breath, slow myself down, and be in contact with God. It is always available to me. Then I feel the serenity that I had when I was meditating and feel calmer, no matter what is happening.

∿

My sponsor taught me that Steps Ten through Twelve are the "maintenance" Steps. My program works better when I don't "should" on myself and when I treat myself with gentleness and kindness. Living with pain and illness is already difficult, and it makes no sense to make it any harder on myself.

In Step Eleven, I prayed and asked to receive the "spiritual virtues of life." They pertain to all aspects of my life, in my relationship with myself and my relationships with others. This is what I pray for daily: courtesy, respect, understanding, forgiveness, love, integrity, humility, honesty, patience, acceptance, and wondrous gratitude. This daily prayer and contact with my Higher Power is how I continue to grow spiritually. Planting these thoughts in my mind lays the seeds of happiness on my life's journey. In this way, I am a friend and not an enemy to myself, as well as to everyone I encounter throughout each day.

This Step helps me to live *One Day at a Time* and to stay in the now. It reminds me to bring the new me into the world on a daily basis. I remember to have an *Attitude of Gratitude* for all my blessings and I say, "Thank you, God. Thank you, God."

Step Twelve

Having had a spiritual awakening as the result of these steps, we tried to carry this message to others who live with chronic pain and illness, and to practice these principles in all our affairs.

Ingredients

Transformation
Recognition of our spiritual awakening
Dedication to a new way of life
Service
Life on life's terms
Purpose and focus
Authenticity
Serenity
Contentment
Gratitude
Discovery of meaning in one's life

Description

Now that we have conscious contact with a Higher Power daily, there will be an awakening. This is a guarantee of the Twelve Steps. It may be gradual or sudden, and it may have occurred already, but one thing is certain: it will feel good—we will feel in harmony with the Universe. Our thoughts and actions have been changed, and our recovery will be evident in our lives. It manifests in many different forms. What is most important is that our obsession with our chronic illness and pain is diminishing or even gone.

Our shift in perspective is from what can we *get* to what can we *give*. We are now asking how we can contribute to the world in a positive way. Others may see the changes in us, possibly even before we recognize them. We have tapped into new resources and no longer feel alone and desperate.

We are proof that miracles can happen. In this Step, we rediscover the joy of living. We have a new state of consciousness. There is an alteration in our lives and ourselves that is tangible. Perceptions, attitudes, and behaviors are transformed.

This is a highly personal experience, yet we will notice a radical change, an overall metamorphosis in the way we see the world and relate to the world. Some of us have a flash of insight that could be called a "spiritual awakening." For many of us, our spiritual awakening is of the more gradual kind. Slowly, we become aware that our response to life's challenges is different. Some of our fears and burdens have been lessened or even removed. We find that we love our life and are happy more often than not.

If, by Step Twelve, we don't feel we've had a spiritual awakening, we can look back through our Steps and check our recipe. Did we use all the ingredients? Did we add any ingredients not called for? This Recipe for Recovery works when we follow it. Sometimes, when a cook adds special ingredients to a recipe, they improve it, and sometimes they don't. If we don't get the end result we wanted, we can simply look back over the recipe and see what we've missed or if an ingredient we've added has overpowered the ones called for.

Even if we are living in difficult circumstances, if we do the work, we *will* see an improvement in our lives.

Directions

Through our own experience, we now know this path works. And so, we need to pass it on to others. This is truly the only way we can help ourselves. Carrying the message is how we keep it alive and maturing within us. We maintain our program by being of service.

How do we actively work Step Twelve? First, we need to recognize our spiritual awakening. If we have had a dramatic experience with our Higher Power and feel new and different, we remember it. We acknowledge it and share about it at meetings and with other members of CPA. If we have had no such "parting of the clouds" experience, we notice situations that used to upset us, that caused us to relapse, or that increased our pain or symptoms for some reason are no longer bothersome. We acknowledge those experiences as evidence of both our own work and our Higher Power doing for us what we could not do for ourselves. These moments make it clear that we are different. By not ignoring them or taking them for granted, we will be aware of what may in fact be *our* version of a spiritual awakening—one that was, and still is, going on. This is spiritual progress. For all of us who work the Steps in this program, such progress will continue as we keep on working and sharing the Steps with others.

One way to acknowledge these moments is to make a gratitude list. When we note what we are grateful for, it increases our joy. Gratitude is one way to encounter our spiritual awakening and recognize it clearly.

How do we work with others? Just as we were sponsored, we sponsor those who are new to the program or who, like us, wish to maintain this way of life. The Twelve Steps use the pronoun "we" because we do this work together, not in isolation. When we continue to help others who need to be guided through the Steps and practice our new behaviors—as we have identified and committed to them—in all the areas of our lives, we bring this healthy way of being to all those we encounter. We add to the good orderly direction, not only of our own lives but of the entire world we inhabit.

Countless small and large miracles are the result of being of service to others and practicing these principles in all our affairs. Where once there may have been discord between ourselves and our loved ones, as we participate in their lives in less self-serving ways, we may be happily surprised by new behaviors in the people and institutions around us. Even when all circumstances are exactly as they were before we had these principles and tools to guide us, we find ourselves content, in harmony, in less pain, and less symptomatic—no matter what anyone else is doing or saying. This is miracle enough. It is what we had been hoping for but perhaps had decided could never come about.

The gratitude we feel at having reached such a place of serenity naturally leads us to share this path with others who may need it.

As is sometimes said, it is a simple path, though not always easy. What makes it possible, even enjoyable, is that we do it together.

This Step is also saying that our work is ongoing. We have adopted a new way of being: living life on life's terms and being of service. It's not a course we took and are now done with. On any given day, if our pain and illness are pulling our attention back toward obsessing and rumination on the negative, we may forget that we have a Higher Power who loves us completely and will help us. We need to reach out to others—to ask for help for ourselves and to be there for others when they are confused and lost. Both are ways to be of service. We need one another to remind us of how far we have come; who we are now; where we want to go, one day at a time; and that we are all in it together.

For many of us, as we began our Step journey, we were plagued with thoughts and questions about whether we were of value and benefit to our family, community, or society. But now, guided by our Higher Power, we find purpose. We discover opportunities to create, to work or contribute in a myriad of ways. We have the sense that we belong and are no longer separate from others. Sometimes our new way of being in the world, based on spiritual principles, guided by love, acceptance, tolerance, forgiveness, understanding and service, inspires those around us. Our transformation is a message of hope.

We know we are not alone, that there is a Power greater than ourselves that we can rely on through any challenge. By carrying the Steps into all our affairs, we demonstrate faith, strength, and wisdom, no matter what life may present to us. We share about the Steps with other members in CPA and carry them in word and deed into all the relationships in our lives. When we pass the Steps on to a fellow member, we are reinforcing them in our own lives, ensuring we consistently practice them in all our affairs. *To keep it, we give it away.*

Through the support of the fellowship and our Step work, we feel safe to be ourselves. In authenticity, we now have the opportunity to be who we were meant to be in this lifetime. That may be something we thought we had to let go of because of our chronic pain and illness. By working these Twelve Steps, we *recover* our true selves, who our Higher Power intended us to be, and now we get to share that with others.

Working the Step

1. What does "spiritual awakening" mean to me? What are some indications that I have had a spiritual awakening? If I have not had an awakening, am I willing to trust that I will?

2. What am I grateful for in my life?

3. How does service work benefit my spiritual growth?

4. What Twelfth Step work did I do this week?

5. How have the Twelve Steps transformed my life? How have they transformed me?

6. In what ways do I practice the principles in all areas of my life?

7. How is my relationship and understanding of my chronic pain and illness different today after working the Twelve Steps?

8. How does passing it on help me keep my recovery?

9. Do I reach out when I need help? How is this of service to others?

10. Am I a good example of CPA recovery? If not, what do I need to do to improve my program?

11. How do I carry the message of recovery? What is the message I carry?

What It Looks Like

One thing about illness—I go round and round, obsessing and trying to control this symptom and that symptom, and that can be its own insanity. Service is getting out of myself through a wide variety of activities. For example, I can be in my own home and chair a phone meeting. When I do service, I am stepping out of myself and connecting with others. Through that connection comes a spiritual feeling, filled with love, and I can't do that by myself. This is what Step Twelve is about, a spiritual awakening, and bringing this message to others helps me as well as them. I feel more connected and less alone than I have been in all the nineteen years I've been disabled from illness.

～

The skepticism I first brought to CPA was strong, and I couldn't see how this program would be able to change my life for the better. But at that point, I had nothing more to lose, so I gave it my all and dove in. I felt very alone, broken in body and in spirit. Today my life is filled with good people, a happy home, and joy for living. I know there are people who feel as low and hopeless as I did when I arrived at my first meeting. They look at me and see the smiling, friendly person I am today, and I want them to know it was not always like this and that they, too, can be happy.

～

The CPA program works, but we have to work it. We have no message to carry to others unless we have worked the Steps and allowed the process to work us. I've heard said in meetings, "Don't quit five minutes before the miracle." I've experienced many miracles as the result of CPA in my life and seen the same in the lives of my friends in the fellowship. Did my illness and pain go away? No. Did my life improve? Yes! This is the message I want to share with others and encourage them to hang in there.

∼

When I started to learn about the Twelve Steps and what recovery meant, I began to do service. First, with service to myself by deciding to give CPA a chance and finding a sponsor to help me work the Steps. From then on, it was a process of learning what true service meant: to myself, my Higher Power, and finally, the CPA fellowship.

∼

Giving away what I have learned allows me to continue to grow in my recovery. Working this Step has a sense of selfishness to it. What I mean by that is, by working with another person with chronic pain or illness, I also grow and my own sense of freedom is enhanced. When any of us starts a meeting in person or on the phone, we are doing that to also help ourselves. We get more out of the meetings by being of service than the newcomer does by being at their first meeting. This Step is the true beauty of this program.

∼

I had the opportunity to work Step Twelve one evening after having a very stressful day at work. Even though my body was screaming, "Go to bed, rest, nurture me," I picked up the phone and returned a call from someone in the throes of their chronic pain and illness. It took the focus off of me and put the focus on someone else. Much to my surprise, it relieved my misery, and I felt much better after I hung up the phone.

~

Doing service or carrying the message can be as simple as sharing our experiences at a meeting. There seem to be an endless amount of opportunities to help the next person who is hurting or struggling with their pain and illness. Just sharing what a terrible day I had can draw others out to share about their own awful day. It alleviates the suffering when we know we are not alone or the only one. Hearing about how someone else got through a challenging day using program tools can make me a little less willing to give up.

~

I have some doctors who are friendly to the CPA program, and I talk to them about what CPA does for me. One doctor lets me put our program brochures in his waiting room. I leave packets for people, and I check them when I go there and add new ones. I've seen people pick them up. This is one way I get the message to others.

~

I reach out to newcomers and get their phone number and give them mine. If they are having a hard time, I call them and see how they are doing. That is the service I can do right now.

~

In Twelve-Step programs, "two-stepping" is jumping from Step One to Step Twelve, with very little time spent on the Steps in between. With time, I have learned that there are two other very important phrases in Step Twelve and that the ability to carry the message is the *result* of *having had a spiritual awakening* and having worked the other Steps to the best of my ability so that I've incorporated the principles found there *in all my affairs.*

~

When we start to practice these principles in all our affairs, we find a life free of entanglements and false steps. We are able to lift our head high, knowing we are being the best person we can possibly be, regardless of our condition. We are learning to live our lives to our fullest potential. This Step reaffirms our life and replenishes our vitality. That is why this Step is our program's lifeblood.

Conclusion

The key to this program is to *Keep It Simple* and to work together. We need to practice gentleness and compassion, keeping in mind that there are no bad people, just people who are in pain and ill and who are suffering.

We learn that we can't think our way into right living, but we can act our way into right thinking. We need to take the actions and put the Steps to work in every moment of our lives. An oak tree cannot grow from a fir seed. Where we place our attention is the seed we are planting today. That is what will grow tomorrow. What kind of tomorrow do we want?

With the guidance of our Higher Power, this is a program of new patterns of perception and being—of transformed thoughts and actions. It makes possible what we thought was not: to see ourselves as men and women deserving of love and kindness and happiness, living expansive, meaningful lives. It is a recipe for renewal, for joy, contentment, and belief in ourselves and others, which many of us had thought was lost forever.

May you find what you need, and far more than you could have imagined, in the Twelve Steps of CPA.

Stories of CPA Recovery

Chronic Pain Anonymous was created in 2004. Since then, many people have benefited from the tools and principles of our program based on the Steps described in this book. In the stories that follow, the men and women of CPA share their personal journeys on the path to recovery from the hardships of chronic pain and chronic illness. They describe how this simple spiritual program improved their lives, showing them the way to live "peacefully, joyfully and comfortably with ourselves, and others."

Using the Tools and the Fellowship of CPA

My chronic pain has progressed over the years. As a result, I have had many new challenges to face. My chronic back pain is caused by scoliosis (a degenerative disc disease), with structural disc slippage in my lower back that sends shooting pain down my leg. I never know how much pain I will be in, but I do know that long periods of sitting, standing, and walking can all be very difficult for me. I have managed to stay employed as a teacher and am very grateful for CPA, which is helping me develop strategies that make working feasible.

Several years ago, I was visiting my mother in another state and we had gone to a used book sale. I just happened to pick up Martha Cleveland's book, *Chronic Illness and the Twelve Steps: A Practical Approach to Spiritual Resilience.* While reading it, I remember thinking, "Wow, could this really work?" I had witnessed the Twelve Steps working with other problems, but would it work with chronic pain? Needless to say, I started devouring the book and considering the concepts. It wasn't too long after that when I heard about a CPA meeting in my town.

When I started the program, there was much discussion of surrender, and I really struggled with that. I had a negative way of looking at the idea of "surrender" in relation to my chronic pain. I thought of it as submission and giving up any responsibility or hope for change in my well-being. It took a lot of prayer, journaling, and talking with my sponsor to move past these feelings. The meetings and literature kept taking me back to the power of surrender . . . so I basically surrendered to the idea of surrendering. This led me to a new level of awakened relief.

I have always had chronic pain, but in the last eight years it has amped up more, seemingly increasing with each passing year. Consequently, I have to keep deepening my recovery. About the time my chronic pain was really kicking in, and my quality of life was really going downhill, my two grown sons moved out of state. This broke my heart, because the pain was so intense and unpredictable I couldn't fathom how I would be able to make trips to see them. I didn't want to stop living and doing the activities that mattered to me, like traveling to be with family. Because I work the CPA program, I can gladly say I visit my sons at least once a year.

With my new understanding, travel looks a little different. Sometimes when I fly, I have to ask for special treatment on the airlines, which might mean they have to classify me as "disabled." Oh well! At times I have had to choose pricier hotels to get a few special treatments that help me deal with my insomnia, which is a side effect of my illness. I have a very supportive husband who "gets it." Not to say he always has, but he tries to be accepting of that pad on the bed, the special seat on the plane, and changing the plan if it means sitting in the car for too many hours.

Before CPA, I put a lot of emphasis on the way I looked. I let myself be defined by my clothes, seeking to be fashionable. The heels are long gone. Now it's all about comfort. Just in the last year, my sponsor and I had to evaluate my clothing and shoe selection. My job requires me to get up early, and I never know what condition I may be in. Did I sleep well? Did I have to take medicine and therefore am I groggy and irritable? I just never know. So I've had to simplify my wardrobe: a few pairs of comfortable slacks that go well with anything and a few outfits I can throw on without any thought.

Also, my body has changed over the years. I'm not always pleased with the changes, but I no longer want to send my body any negative messages. I want to celebrate all that my body does well and have compassion and love for what doesn't work as well.

This program has shed a whole new light on what taking care of myself means. I have a very active and outdoorsy family, and they are not always open to my declining an outing or my need to go slower or simply stay behind. In CPA, I learned I have permission to slow down, rest if needed, meditate, be in nature, or whatever it takes to be kind and loving to myself. Honoring myself, honoring my needs, and learning how to take care of myself has been life-altering. Being OK with the fact that my needs change, because the level of pain doesn't always stay the same, is vital to my well-being. For example, taking care of myself sometimes means making the choice to cancel an afternoon commitment in order to save my energy for an evening event.

I am a strong believer in working the Steps, going to meetings (either face-to-face or phone meetings), and checking in with my sponsor regularly. The thoughts and emotions surrounding chronic pain and illness, if kept in my own head, can make me crazy. Instead, I have been able to retrain my thought processes in so many helpful ways using the Steps, the tools, and the fellowship of CPA.

I use the phone to check in with my program friends who also deal with chronic pain issues. My mind can go pretty squirrely dealing with medications, supplements, treatments, doctors, and insurance companies. Recently, I had to switch doctors, and having someone to talk through it with was so comforting. It helped to share my concerns about building a new relationship with another doctor, having to tell my story again, and wanting to be open to new ideas but still staying true to my beliefs. It's a balancing act, and not everyone gets it. All of this would be overwhelming without the fellowship of CPA.

Even though my chronic pain has progressed over the years, which has brought many new challenges, I have grown spiritually and emotionally. I "stayed around for the miracle," which means I kept coming back to meetings and working the program, even when I wanted to give up. As a result, I can celebrate many victories, including having a life that is full of love for myself and others.

Hope for the Future

At the age of twenty-nine, right in the middle of my last semester of nursing school, I noticed a problem with my eyes. My vision was blurred and was worsening every day. I saw an ophthalmologist who thought that I had a brain tumor. After several tests, including an MRI, I was diagnosed with multiple sclerosis (MS). That was sixteen years ago. Since then, I have been on an emotional and physical roller coaster, which is typical for MS. I was handling my limitations pretty well until a few years ago when I began to have severe pain in my neck and feet. My neurologist noted three ruptured discs in my neck and an MS lesion in my cervical spine.

The doctors told me there was a fifty-fifty chance that the pain I was experiencing was either from the lesion or the ruptured discs. I took a chance and had surgery to address these problems. After a three-month recovery, the pain in my feet and neck returned. I was devastated. My pain doctor told me that I could not work again as a nurse and that I shouldn't be working at all. He also told me that there was nothing that he could do to totally alleviate my pain and that I would have this pain for the rest of my life.

I was supposed to accept both the fact that I was never going to work as a nurse again and that I would be in pain for the rest of my life. In my search for relief, I tried every pain medication known to man. I tried yoga, meditation, hypnosis, herbal therapies, and exercise, none of which worked for me. I found myself in a hopeless state and began spiraling into a deep depression.

My pain syndrome became exacerbated to the point that I was in agonizing pain most of the time. After a couple of medication changes, I felt little relief and knew that I had to find some way to deal with the increase in pain. At one point, I even attempted suicide. When I saw my daughter look into my eyes and say, "Why would you want to leave me?," I began to turn my life around. My life was headed down the wrong path, and her words were a wake-up call.

One day, I was surfing the Internet for a group to help me deal with my pain. I thought there must be something out there for people who suffer from chronic pain. I believe that my Higher Power intervened, and I found CPA. I am very familiar with Twelve-Step programs, as I have seen firsthand how they have helped my friends and family members.

CPA has been one of the few things that helped me live with my illness and deal with the pain that I have every day. I personally believe that a good attitude is 50 percent of the healing process for any illness. Talking with others who know what it is like to live with pain and being reminded to "hang in there" on the bad days improves my attitude and makes me feel that I am not alone. I need the members of CPA for this kind of support.

I have a wonderful fiancé, and I have family and friends who love and care for me, but they don't know what it's like to live with this pain every day. My heart goes out to my fiancé and all the other caregivers and partners that feel helpless sharing a life with a person with chronic pain. I can only imagine what it's like to constantly see the person you love in pain. These caring, giving people in our lives want us to be out of pain. My being a member of CPA has helped my fiancé indirectly, because now I can talk to people who understand my struggles and that helps *me* feel better. My mental pain has been eased through attending meetings, reading the literature, and hearing how others work the program. CPA has changed my life and the lives of my loved ones and has given me hope for the future.

If I never had MS or chronic pain in my life, I would never have the appreciation for life I have right now. Every time I look at my daughters, I thank God that I didn't go through with suicide and decided to stick around and fight. I thank God for every day he gives me, for the hope that things can improve, and for the people in my life who love and care about me. God has given me so much for which to be thankful. Every time I get depressed, I turn to my HP to ask for strength to accept the powerlessness I have over my illness and gratitude for all the gifts I have been given.

I recently attended my daughter's wedding. I was dancing and celebrating with her, even though I was wracked with pain. I wouldn't have missed that experience for anything. I know that I am powerless over my illness, and I accept that. If I am able to do just one thing that I like to do each day, it's a victory for me. Occasionally I have a day when I don't have pain, and for that I am most grateful. I will probably never be out of pain completely, but I will never stop choosing to carry on.

Sharing Our Courage, Strength, and Hope during Difficult Times

Observing the positive changes in a couple of friends with chronic illness and pain inspired me to give CPA a try. Over a period of years, I'd watched them struggle through the challenges, complexities, and fears of dealing with chronic disease and chronic pain. I couldn't help but notice the changes in them.

They seemed to embody the Serenity Prayer: *God, grant me the serenity to accept the things I cannot change, the courage to change the things I can, and the wisdom to know the difference.* They had discovered a healthier, happier way of life, despite what they and modern medicine couldn't change.

At my first meeting, I shared about my ongoing struggle with posttraumatic stress disorder (PTSD) and the resulting severe physiological side effects. I'd witnessed a fatal accident as a toddler, lost someone dear to me, and was injured myself. The untreated injury caused lifelong pain that increased through the years, despite numerous medical attempts to correct it.

My healing team, consisting of medical doctors, counselors for PTSD, physical therapists, and clergy, helped me deal with the trauma to my body, mind, and spirit.

Insurance didn't cover much of the necessary treatments, thus requiring me to use most of my assets. This included giving up my home and using the equity to survive. My ability to continue working was limited, as standing for any length of time was no longer feasible.

Once the acute phase of my PTSD responded to the treatments, I needed to deal with the reality of the remaining chronic pain and physical disease. The isolation I was in as a result of my limited functions seemed to intensify the chronic pain, and fear magnified this. On the surface, I looked "fine." Even family and friends didn't understand why I couldn't "just get over it." Too often, neither did I.

I came to understand that my physical healing process would continue for the rest of my life and that there would be mental, emotional, and spiritual challenges as well. There were episodes of extreme pain from the old injuries and changes in my body as the result of years of medication to treat that pain. With dark humor, I described my condition as "scrambled brains and scrambled body."

I reached out to the members of CPA and was directed to the website and invited to the local meeting. What a relief! Here were others who had ongoing challenges, even though their specific conditions were different than mine. These people understood what it meant to cope every day with chronic conditions and they cared. This was a safe place to be open and honest about all my feelings.

Most of all, everyone was committed to *sharing our courage, strength, and hope*, even when the going got rough. When my courage faltered, the CPA program and the fellowship encouraged me to surrender and risk trusting my Higher Power to help me begin again, no matter how far down a setback seemed to take me.

Feelings of shame at being unable to live as I believed I must, in order to be worthy, gave way to knowing my own value and usefulness. Even when in the depth of pain and despair, I learned it's possible to listen with kindness, to myself and others. I can be present with acceptance, compassion, and love, though I may be bedridden and in severe pain, because I received this gift from others in program.

When my own energy isn't enough to get through the next moment, slogans such as *One Day at a Time* and *Progress, Not Perfection* remind me that I am just fine exactly as I am right now. The slogans provide *courage* when I need it, especially to recognize and halt harmful cycles of negative self-talk. Reading in CPA literature how others have used their program reminds me I am not alone, and this knowledge gives me fortitude to go on.

I believe I'd never have survived my PTSD and chronic pain without God, the mysterious Power greater than the traumatized, wounded child who still lives within me. And still, at times when the pain is most intense, remembering this Power greater than any human seems far out of reach. When I choose to take a Step, make a phone call, or text or e-mail my sponsor or a program friend, I am reminded that God is right there. This helps me reconnect to the *strength* of the Spirit within me.

Last, but not least, is *hope*. When I feel hopeless, it's a reminder to reach out and ask to be accepted just as I am. This is when I most need to let go of all the isolating behaviors I've used to defend against feeling vulnerable, needy, and imperfect. Over and over again, I learn to ask for what I need and be open to receive it. Hope comes back into my life when I take action and reach out for support.

As I work my program, solutions I never imagined begin to appear, and the quality of my life improves. With the help of my Higher Power, the next right action comes without struggle. Connections to other people on the recovery journey have brought me a wonderful roommate, ideas that have led to financial assistance, and renewed energy. My feelings of shame and fear and my habit of isolation have been replaced with love, gratitude, and community. These are the gifts of CPA.

From Anger to Serenity

I screamed at people throughout the first three years of my chronic pain and illness. Even people who wanted to help me! I was either screaming or sobbing. It's interesting to remember that because things have changed so much for me. It's not that I don't ever get obnoxiously angry now—I do, and I notice that I am still more prone to anger than I used to be before I had chronic pain and illness. But it really does happen so much less often, and I feel so terrible after an angry outburst that I have to call my sponsor and then make an amends. So now, I try to catch it before it happens. It makes my life a lot more pleasant and a lot easier if I can feel my anger without expressing it and hurting people.

It was a couple years of attending CPA meetings before I began to take the Steps with my sponsor. When I began that work, I experienced a rebirth. Everything in my life became uncannily laid out before me by my Higher Power: opportunities started to happen that I never imagined would happen, and new experiences and new people entered my life.

Taking Step One and admitting that I was powerless over chronic pain and illness led to waking up one day with the thought that I was never going to get better until I understood what was going on in my body. I felt like I had taken my power back—not by trying to change the chronic pain but by accepting it and even trying to learn something about it.

Serenity did not come all at once. I spent several years being extremely anxious about my life. I could only work part time and could not do many things that had given me pleasure before becoming ill, like running, being with friends, and going out to dinner and the movies. It took a while before I could even walk for ten minutes and a long time before I was willing to live with the pain that going to dinner and the movies brings me. But gradually, the pain became just a fact of my life. I discovered that sometimes when I was really terrified to do something—like travel to London—I would get there and end up having much less pain than I have in my regular life at home.

It was surprising to see that I could in fact be returned to sanity. This meant I could live a life that had purpose and meaning, even with chronic pain and illness. My health condition did not have to mean absolute isolation and despair. There have been many difficult things—because life does bring difficult things—but the stronger my connection to my Higher Power becomes, the more serene I become. One day at a time, I see the possibility that I will be all right. My Higher Power really will not forsake me, no matter what life brings.

I'm on Steps Eight and Nine, and I'm finding them a real challenge. Here's a recent example. I bought some new walking shoes (I can walk for several miles now) and I wasn't sure about them, but the sales clerk said I could return them if they didn't work out. I did return them the next day, but when the saleswoman asked me if I had walked outside in them, I said no—even though in fact I had walked outside. She accepted my story and my return of the shoes. I immediately knew I had to call my sponsor. We talked and it was clear: I had to go back to the store and make amends. I have to tell the truth, whatever the consequences may be. So I'm very embarrassed, but I look forward to going back, telling the truth, and being the kind of person I want to be.

What's really unexpected is that today my life is all about "how" I am as a person—honest, open, and willing—*not* about my chronic pain and illness. So, in fact, chronic pain and illness brought me the gift of becoming a better human being.

Pain Does Not Control My Life

After a year of suffering with a variety of symptoms and medical tests showing nothing wrong, I was finally diagnosed with fibromyalgia. My pain was extreme, and I was often in tears as the pain increased, in part because I was trying to continue to live the life I'd been used to living for over fifty years. Seeking relief, I got massages, chiropractic care, a good medical doctor and tried many pain prescriptions, but there was little improvement. I didn't know what else to do. To suddenly and unexpectedly change from being independent and capable of living what I considered a normal life to being unable to keep up with my responsibilities and customary recreation was devastating. I was miserable.

On most days, driving home from work I was in tears because of the pain. I would go home and collapse for about thirty minutes and then drag myself out of bed so that I could help make dinner. If I tried to mop a floor, I hurt so much for days afterwards that I could hardly believe it. My days required constant, brief intervals of resting so that I could get back up and work or do whatever I needed to do.

I ran after any promising possibility of help or hope and saw a lot of money go down the drain as I tried anything that might bring relief. Friends and family offered a lot of advice. Soon I had more options to try than I had time to try them, and I began to doubt that anything would make a difference.

I heard of CPA from a friend in another Twelve-Step fellowship, and I made contact with someone who was a member of CPA. She spoke so happily of how CPA had changed her life from one of misery and suffering to a wonderful, full one that I was instantly intrigued. I'm a little embarrassed to say that I seriously considered the possibility that this group could magically take away my illness and pain, that they had discovered a wonderful secret. I went to my first meetings with the idea that maybe these people had found some miraculous way of healing—maybe mind over matter or positive thinking. Part of me knew that wasn't likely, but another part of me longed for this to be the case. This is how I began my adventure with this transformative program.

As you may have guessed, there was no magical, miraculous method of healing my body. There was something equally wonderful, though, and maybe even better. I began a journey of learning to trust my own Higher Power, take care of myself, and show up every day for a life that is meaningful and satisfying.

The first tool that made a big difference in my life was the Three *A*s: awareness, acceptance, and action. Awareness meant observing and acknowledging what my body felt like and how certain activities made me feel, both physically and emotionally. Acceptance was the next step. Acceptance did *not* mean that I gave up and decided that I was ill and in pain and that was all there was to it, that there was nothing I could do. It meant looking at reality and seeing what was true.

By accepting my "new normal," I was then able to move to the next "A": action. Because I accepted how I felt and how my body had changed, I was able to take appropriate action. The constant struggle to keep up with my former lifestyle only led to more emotional and physical pain. Some examples of action for me were giving up my position with my company and moving to a lower status, part-time position; getting help with housework and learning to accept a home not as clean as I would really like; taking ten to twenty trips from my car to carry groceries into the house instead of two or three, because I could not carry much weight at one time, or alternately, having someone else unload the groceries; learning to say no to things I used to do, such as helping with family moves or babysitting grandchildren by myself; and having others share the work of holiday family dinners. I had to say good-bye to bicycling for miles and be content with mild walking for exercise. These decisions, along with many more along the way, have resulted in much less pain.

These changes were not easy. It was wrenching to give up my position at work because I had worked so hard to attain it. It was also difficult to give up the income and the satisfaction I felt by contributing financially to our household. It was surprising how much of my identity was tied up in my job and what I did in life. I struggled with guilt and had the feeling that I was no longer carrying my weight and doing my fair share in many areas of my life. Saying no to the activities I once enjoyed was difficult and still is, but it is getting easier because it just makes good sense.

These decisions and choices were good because I was doing what my mind and body needed, but on the other hand, they were not good because I began to feel useless and worthless. This brings me to another wonderful lesson I learned through CPA: I am just as valuable ill as I was healthy. God loves me just as much now as he did before. I am a human *being*, not a human doing. I can still contribute to this world and my family. I've just had to learn new ways of doing so. This is turning into a great adventure of discovery.

I am learning to trust in my Higher Power more and more. I am becoming happier in ways I never would have if my life had not taken this turn. I rose to meet new challenges in my life and took unexpected paths, such as starting my own business. It never would have entered my mind to start my own business if illness hadn't driven me to leave my former employment. In my new career, I have been able to experience the satisfaction of seeing what I could accomplish on my own, with God's help and guidance. This experience has helped me grow and has been a thrilling ride!

There have been times of grief and depression, but these are to be expected. In CPA, I learned that I have experienced loss and that it is OK to grieve. When depression and grief seem to be taking over too much, I learn from the phrase "Gratitude is the greenhouse of contentment." Making lists, either mentally or in writing, of the things I *can* still do and the blessings in my life, even if I don't feel like making such a list, often results in a positive attitude, overriding the negative. It isn't always that simple, of course, but it is a tool that often helps.

I have been feeling much better lately. It is in part due to the help of a medical practitioner, in part due to the love and care of my husband, and in part due to the things I have learned in CPA. Because I've learned to take care of myself, and that it is good and OK to do so, I have taken note of what makes me feel worse, and I make choices to avoid those things or activities. This has meant that the people I interact with have had to learn new ways of experiencing life with me.

At first this was difficult because I did not want to disappoint them. As my confidence in taking care of myself grew, I became more comfortable living within these guidelines. The benefits were less pain and a happier life. Pain was no longer controlling my life . . . or so I thought.

I discovered I was a little smug about how well my life was going. One day, during a CPA meeting, I saw to my surprise that pain was still insidiously in control in an unexpected way. The guidelines I had set up had become rigid rules that I felt entitled to. By rigorously adhering to these rules, I was denying myself and others some valuable experiences in life. The fear of pain was controlling me by keeping me inside my safe walls and not letting me experience life as fully as I could. It is not good to live life always being careful, so that nothing causes me to hurt more. Sometimes it's OK to choose to take a risk. I may pay a price for the choice, but it could be worth it. Other times, I may be surprised by not having to pay a price. Being inflexible can result in losing out on times of joy.

The slogan *Easy Does It* applies here. I had a good system that became not so good because I overdid it. Learning to balance taking care of myself with living a life that is rich and full, not only for me but also for those whose lives intertwine with mine, is a new challenge. There is always something new to learn, a new way to grow. The slogans and Steps of CPA give me the guidance I need to do that.

Applying the Twelve Steps to my illness was a great relief. Summarized, the first three Steps say, "I can't, God can, I will let

Him." I don't have to strive and wonder and try to figure it all out! I can turn it over to my Higher Power and trust that He wants and knows what is best for me, no matter how it looks to me at the moment.

As someone who is working the Steps in this program, I can confidently say what my CPA friend said: My life has gone from miserable to wonderful and fulfilling, and I have CPA to thank for showing me the way. I don't have to let pain control my life. It is what it is. Yes, I live in fairly constant pain. So what? It's no longer a big deal. I once again enjoy living and giving and loving, and even receiving.

CPA did have a wonderful secret that changed my life—it's just not the one I originally thought it might be. CPA and the Twelve Steps are truly one of the greatest gifts in my life.

Helping Others Helps Me

I was raised by a father who was a hard-working framing contractor and a mother who was very caring. I was always energetic—the middle child, who some people say is the comedian or a person who likes to keep the peace. I was always trying to make people laugh. I was told to work hard and that I could do anything I wanted if I just worked for it. I started working when I was fourteen years old: doing a paper route before school, and washing dishes at night after school. When I got paid, I loved to help the family pay our bills, as by then my parents were divorced and I was helping Mom raise my brothers.

High school was not for me. I took the GED and joined the military. I wanted to work on airplanes, on jets in particular, but when I got out of the military, the economy was so depressed that I joined the construction union. I started as an apprentice, using a jackhammer in a ditch. Soon I started my own business, and I worked without missing a day, including weekends, because, to me, that was the way to be. People really looked up to me, and I liked that. Some nights I would come home just exhausted, my back hurting badly and my legs starting to give me problems. Whatever I did, I wanted to look good, no matter what it put my body through. I felt like Superman.

I started a company building custom homes, and then, my back gave way and I had to go to the hospital. The doctors told me that I had to have a spinal fusion, but I didn't care, as I thought I was invincible at that time. I had the surgery and back to work I went. Before you knew it, I was on my job site and already working before the stitches were even out of my back.

A few years later, business slowed down, so I went to work for a finishing company and was rushing around trying to get stuff done—trying to show how much I could do. A 200-pound board fell from the 16-foot ceiling, hitting me in the head and breaking the vertebrae in my neck and also damaging my right arm and shoulder. I remember being told to stay still, and all I wanted to do was get up. To the hospital I went again, and they gave me a single-level fusion of the neck and rebuilt my right shoulder.

The pain when I woke up was really bad this time. I was older and was not recovering like I did in the past. I tried to work again and the screws loosened in my neck, which led to my second neck surgery. I remember being really nervous about this surgery. Just before going in, I asked the doc if I was going to be OK. He said, "I do this all the time, you will be fine." I awoke different this time. I had trouble breathing, and I was moving all over and couldn't control it. The doctors didn't know it at the time, but in cutting across the front of my neck, they had paralyzed my left phrenic nerve, lifting my left hemidiaphragm and paralyzing my left lung—giving me phrenic nerve palsy.

They cut me loose from care after a few weeks, and I started a new career. I went to school to become a building inspector and to get my real estate license. But I found myself in a bad market again. So I went back to work in construction, only to end up in the emergency room one more time. I had loose hardware in my neck and needed another level of fusion. This time, they went in through the back of my neck. Eight more screws were added to the six I already had in the front, making that fourteen screws total in my neck.

When I awoke, I had no memory to speak of and the pain was unreal. Even staying still, I hurt horribly down my arms and in my chest. I had lost everything by this time: my homes and my construction company. I couldn't do building inspection because I couldn't look up or down much at all. I had lost all hope of ever having any type of life worth living. At this time, I was living in a hotel with just one suitcase. My sons were very upset and my family did not understand what was happening to me, and I wished they could. I was gone, inside and out.

Out of the blue, my insurance company called me and sent me to see a pain psychologist. This doctor helped put in place a team of doctors—a neurologist, a pulmonary doctor, a pain doctor, and himself—with a case manager to oversee it all. They found all the issues that were present and started to address them.

All I could think about was how to get rid of my pain and have my old life back. My psychologist suggested to me that my life (as I once knew it) might be gone. I felt totally hopeless and helpless. That was my bottom right there. I really thought that my life was truly over. I couldn't just bounce back from this. I was cornered and scared. I looked at the doctor and he said, "We are going to work on getting you a new purpose for living." (Later on, the Steps would help me find a life worth living *with* my disabilities.)

Then, while doing an online search about pain, I stumbled across CPA on a website. It looked like it could be exactly what I needed, so I started a face-to-face meeting at the local hospital. Five to six patients met every week. We would talk of a better way of thinking in order to cope with our pain. Some were ready, some were not, but I certainly was. I was tired of living like I had been. We registered the group on the CPA website and started a book-study meeting. From that point, my life kept getting better. I was now showing up for something bigger than me, and it gave me a purpose, a reason to leave my room.

I believed in a Higher Power, and I had come to call him "God." But I didn't feel him at the time. I knew about the Twelve-Step programs; I went to AA meetings with my father as a child and have been sober in AA for twenty-three years, but it never occurred to me to use them for my pain. Now I was desperate enough to try. I started with acceptance and recognizing that my life was unmanageable. I had a little trouble accepting some of my physical problems, but I knew for sure that my life was unmanageable. That was Step One.

When I fully accepted all my problems and understood I would be like this from now on, I started to look for a Higher Power again, especially to help during my lowest points. I noticed that whenever I either talked of God or read about recovery, my pain would become more manageable, even lessen, and become more livable. When I was agitated, my pain would fly through the roof. When I saw this pattern clearly, I *came to believe*, right there—Step Two. My next question was, how do I control this? I still wanted to control the situation.

Still trying to manage things, I found myself in fear very often. When the fear would come, the pain would get horrible. I didn't medicate those spikes of pain. That just created other kinds of pain, so I turned to God again for the *fear*. I found he would take fear from me when I gave up trying to control it. That's when I stumbled on letting go and doing the next right thing. I would say, "God, you can handle this fear; I am going to do the dishes. Talk to ya later," and I noticed my pain would lessen enough to do the dishes. I had to pay attention to remember to do this, which was hard—I had a severed nerve root and two nerves pinched in my neck, and my breathing was bad. Still, daily I *made a decision* to turn my fear and my pain over to God as I understood Him—Step Three.

As time went on, I found it absolutely necessary to be honest with my doctors—about the medications and all my activities—if I was to expect the health professionals to be able to help me. That realization came to me after doing my inventory in Step Four.

My mother passed away several years ago. That was one of the hardest days in my recovery. I still showed up at my meeting for CPA. I was able to manage my pain without turning to medication, but my thinking went up and down. Still, I used what I knew at the time to help me through all that pain. And it worked.

A couple of years ago, I had respiratory failure and was back in the hospital. This time the doctors gave me a left thoracotomy, trying to stabilize my lung. I had friends in the program now that were there for me. I was no longer alone. My family showed up, too. Working the Steps got me through that one, and I recovered from it faster for that reason.

My expectations—how I used to want my family to react to my pain and my not being able to do certain things—have now changed. I no longer want them to know how I feel; that would mean they would have what I have. I would not want that. I just simply say "yes" when I mean yes and "no" when I mean I can't do it. I don't feel guilt anymore. That is a miracle. They accept me now, as I am, and I do the best I can with them.

I have recreated my life through the Steps of CPA. As I work this program of action, I have a new purpose in life that becomes more fulfilling every day.

I never dreamed when I was younger that I would be helping other people in order to save myself, but that is what is happening. It's been five years since I started that first CPA group. Now I have a meeting at my house and a meeting at the hospital where we share our experience, strength, and hope with other people who suffer from chronic pain and illness. We learn how to live fully, *with* our chronic pain and illness.

It would appear that my purpose, what that doctor so long ago was hoping I'd find, is to help others with chronic pain and illness. I go wherever I am called. When I am reaching out to help another, not thinking of myself, I'm actually helping myself get better. There is nothing like watching the light go on when you've helped another person recover and find a new way of living. My hope is that if you have lost hope, you too can find a new life through CPA.

Using Pain Medications Responsibly

For many of us in CPA, living with chronic pain and illness is the most difficult thing we have ever dealt with. For me, it is not. In my late twenties, I began to recover memories of the severe psychological and sexual abuse I had experienced as a child. My world turned upside down. I had only recently established a relationship with a Higher Power, and I was thrust into doubt. How could a loving God have let these things happen to me when I was young and vulnerable?

Slowly, my understanding of a loving Higher Power and a universe worth living in expanded to include this painful history. I reached a new level of trust and surrender. I learned that in spiritual matters, the question "why?" is seldom useful. The word "how" is more important. How can I live well in these circumstances? How can I improve my attitude and find peace of mind? How can I accept *what is* instead of focusing on "what should have been"?

This understanding was again challenged when I began to have chronic illness and chronic pain. My active, stimulating life became more and more limited. I advanced from experiencing pain, weakness, and sickness once or twice a week to every single day. Periods of relief were measured in hours or minutes. I became less and less able to work to support myself and eventually had to apply for financial assistance.

Those of us recovering from substance addiction are faced with a challenge when it comes to dealing with pain medication. Some choose not to use it, and I respect that. For me, I do not consider living without pain medication an option. The physical pain is too severe and leads me to thoughts of suicide. There are, however, certain precautions I must take as an addict/alcoholic who needs pain medication.

I am honest with my doctor about my addiction, and I am careful to choose doctors who understand addiction. I make sure that at least one physician knows about every medication I take and, when possible, get them all from the same prescriber. When it is necessary to have another prescriber, as it was when I had two teeth extracted, I send a copy of the new prescription to my primary doctor. Perhaps most importantly, *I follow the instructions* provided, something that never came easily to me. When it is necessary to change a dosage, I clear it with my doctor immediately. I report my daily medication use to another recovering alcoholic. And I occasionally have to remind myself that medication is for physical pain only, *not* emotional pain.

Emotional and spiritual pain are what CPA helps me with the most. Grief, disappointment, frustration, loneliness, isolation, and fear are things I can't and don't have to face alone. The understanding and love of others in recovery, the help of a Higher Power, and the relief of working the Twelve Steps bring those emotions into a manageable range.

Today I am careful how I choose my words and tone of voice when speaking about my pain and illness. When necessary, I report it, but I do not overemphasize the symptoms. I avoid words like "miserable" and "suffering." I may say, "My pain level is high right now," or "I'm not able to walk today," or "I'm feeling very weak." If a friend asks how I'm doing, I often say, "I'm good." For laughs I add, "The new good, not the old good." With the help of CPA, I am again finding a new level of surrender and acceptance.

My Value as a Person Is Not Based on What I Do

It was Christmas Eve morning, and here is what I had planned for the day: work the lights at my church for Christmas Eve services from 3:30 p.m. to 6:30 p.m., go to my aunt's for a potluck later in the evening, help my husband prepare Christmas dinner for fourteen people for tomorrow, and get the house tidied up for tomorrow. That morning, my chronic pain condition flared up, along with a migraine. You can imagine what I felt.

I was very upset, depressed, frustrated, worried, and fearful. I had self-pity and feelings of low self-worth, thinking that I was just a useless sick person. I was full of grief and loneliness. Lying on my bed and crying, lost in despair, down in darkness, I started to struggle to reach out to my program. My first efforts were feeble, but knowing that this program works, and that it could help me overcome much of my emotional pain, kept me from giving up.

I reminded myself, "I am powerless over when the illness strikes. God is in control and can help me through this." I accepted the situation, turned it over to God, and prayed one of my favorite prayers: *God, please help me to have the best day I can under the circumstances.* Remembering that I am a human being, not a human "doing," brought some comfort. My value as a person is not based on what I do.

I was able to detach myself from the emotional storm by observing my emotions and acknowledging their presence. In this way, it became possible for my feelings to be present without letting them run the show.

I didn't know exactly how this holiday weekend was going to end up, but I was trusting God to hold me in His hands and be with me through it. The restoration of sanity in Step Two means not being lost in the whirlwind of painful emotions, and Step Three means peacefully trusting my Higher Power.

If it were not for CPA, I would not have learned these tools. I am very thankful for this program.

I No Longer Feel Alone

I was born into an alcoholic home as the third of four girls. My mother did her best, but it was a far cry from a loving, supportive, accepting, or encouraging home. Instead, it was filled with negative judgments, no hugs, no words like "I love you" spoken, no acknowledgments for deeds well done but plenty of neglect, blame and shame. One night, my mother was so depressed that she loaded a shotgun and was going to kill us all. Luckily, my dad wrestled it out of her hands, leaving a giant hole where she shot through the kitchen floor. My father was no saint. He couldn't have cared less about his children or our grades; he molested all four of his daughters while my mother looked the other way. At the age of fifteen, I "turned him in" to the state where we lived, and he was removed from the home—but allowed to return. At sixteen, I dropped out of high school, lied about my age, and got a factory job to pay for my first apartment. I managed to get a high school diploma by going to school while working at night.

I tell this family-of-origin part of my story because the emotional pain of not having parents capable of love left me learning how to handle significant pain on my own.

I dreamed of becoming a college graduate and having children, but I knew I had to first change the harmful road I was on, which was making it difficult to reach my goals. Thankfully, one of the girls I played softball with was in AA. She took me to my first AA meeting and divine intervention helped me with all the rest.

Five years into my sobriety and having earned my bachelor's degree, almost with honors, I was driving to work in a snowstorm and was hit head-on by an oncoming driver. The injuries sustained, as I was listening to the doctors and nurses at the trauma center discuss them, included adjectives like "crushed," "shredded," "mangled." The worst of it was a shattered pelvis and hip, with a damaged sciatic nerve. They weren't sure I would sit again, let alone walk.

It took many months of surgeries and hard work, in a swimming pool and rehabilitation center, to learn how to sit and walk again. During this time, I continued my education, working from my bed to earn my MBA degree at an online college. Against the odds, I did return to sitting and walking, although I could only do a little of each. I switched careers and went to work for a doctor as the office administrator.

All I could do was work and come home. I lay on my sofa in the evening, exhausted and in pain. That was when I realized I didn't know how to slow down. I almost killed myself trying to keep up with the demands of the job while ignoring my pain and rehabilitation exercises. The stress was severe, and eventually I wound up with a headache that lasted more than eight weeks. The cause was high blood pressure. I had to leave the job and go back on disability—and get back to my rehab exercises.

I decided to move to a new state that had milder weather so I could walk every day and keep my legs and body strong while keeping my body warm. I developed a routine of exercise and meditation. I was learning how to handle living with pain, but living with pain was very isolating. I still went to AA meetings, but I didn't feel like I was a part of the group. I was in too much pain to go out and socialize with others, and it didn't feel like talking about pain would be OK. People didn't understand what it was like living with chronic pain. I desperately needed somebody to talk to about it. No matter how hard I tried to maintain some semblance of what my life used to look like, I just couldn't "keep up" with other people. As I became more and more isolated, I started to consider suicide.

Instead of getting better due to my move, my pain was getting worse. Not only did I hurt where I had been injured in the car accident, but I started to have pain in my feet, hands, and joints. My physical condition was sliding backwards to where I'd started just after the car accident, and nobody could tell me why.

I was collecting disability, but I missed work, and my SSDI wasn't enough, so I joined the SSDI Workforce Development program. They helped me develop new skills and become a broadband connection specialist. I was trained to work from my recliner (since I cannot sit upright) and worked four hours a day, helping customers get connected to the broadband service. It was fun, but sitting (or reclining), along with the stress of the job, made the pain worse. I had many flare-ups that prevented me from working for weeks at a time. Eventually, I had to give up that job, too. I decided to do bookkeeping for local small businesses and did that from my reclining bed, but that also proved to be too hard. I was going downhill. I tried several different jobs from home and learned the skills to do the jobs, but my body just wouldn't cooperate. I had to stop working altogether.

At this point, I hit a physical, emotional, and spiritual bottom. Luckily, I had a sponsor in AA who said that I needed to find a group that could help me learn to live with my new limitations. I realized that I was acting just like an alcoholic and unwilling to admit complete defeat. I didn't want to be mentally and physically different than my peers. I had the idea that if I just worked hard enough, I could "get over" the pain and sickness. The delusion that I am like other "able-bodied" people, or that I am like my old self as an able-bodied person, had to be shattered so that I could see how I was in denial, just like when I was working the Steps in AA.

With my AA sponsor's encouragement, I found CPA, and again, I worked hard. At that time, we had an online meeting. When I read the sharing there and ordered all the literature, I knew I had found my home. Here was a room full of people who also had to let go of who they were and work hard to find out what their new normal was, and is. I had to grieve and accept the loss of finances, lovers, gardening, making stained glass, playing the piano, and sailing. I was able to share my grief with others who were grieving the loss of all kinds of activities and people in their lives. They were just like me and mourning life as they once knew it.

In CPA, I reimagined my Higher Power. I discovered that my Higher Power is simply *love*. My Higher Power would never allow a head-on collision to ruin my life, or horrible diseases to ravage my body, or my family members to abuse me. My Higher Power lives deep within me and helps me whenever I need to quiet or soothe my spirit or to gather strength to face the things I cannot change. My Higher Power has basically become a loving verb.

When I came to CPA and started reading the literature, I got a sponsor and together we worked the Steps. The First Step was the longest and hardest Step I ever took. It opened my eyes to many areas in my life that were unmanageable and where I needed to improve, especially when it comes to being responsible for my behavior when in pain or feeling sick. Working the program with a sponsor helped me to release the shame I felt.

I felt comfortable bringing my sadness and grief to the meetings, even as I lost more of my abilities to function. The CPA group members listened when I shared about the negative changes as they occurred, such as my muscles getting weaker, becoming sun-sensitive, and episodes of paralysis. I felt supported and cared for as I worked to develop ways to adjust to my changing body.

Since coming to CPA, I learned I have lupus, dermatomyositis, fibromyalgia, and Raynaud's disease and was told I can't go out in the sun because it makes me ill. (That felt like a cruel joke, given that I moved to a sunny state to treat the pain from my car accident.) Recently I got a wheelchair, and it's been a godsend, but boy did I fight it! Because I'm a member of CPA, I have other people to talk to as I have been collecting these diagnoses.

It has helped to be *honest* in admitting I have a thinking problem about my pain and illness, to be *open* to sharing it with others in CPA, and to be *willing* to work at applying spiritual principles to solve my thinking problems. I've learned that's the *HOW* in "how it works": honest, open, and willing.

To my utter amazement and forever gratitude, I have, for the most part, let go of the self-pity, and I have no resentments. The more service I do, the less isolated I feel. The more I lean on my Higher Power, the more love I have for myself and willingness to help others. When I stay centered on my Higher Power, my thinking problem about my chronic pain and illness transforms: from self-centered pity and resentment to outward thinking and asking how I might help somebody else, each day.

It's been a real honor to help write literature, watch CPA grow, and observe members grow and change. The best part is that I don't feel alone like I did when I couldn't get out to meetings anymore. I can stay in my recliner and dial in to a meeting any day of the week now. We can even see one another on our video-chat meeting. It is wonderful to be able to see members of our group no matter where we live. People in my meetings understand me, and we help each other to make each day as positive as we possibly can. I'm so grateful for that. Thank you, CPA, for helping me be not so alone and for allowing me the opportunity to be of service,

Suffering Is a State of Mind

Becoming afflicted with a chronic illness was never part of my plans.

Prior to becoming sick, I led a charmed life. I had a happy childhood, grew up, and married my high school sweetheart. We went on to have two gorgeous children who we raised in the dream home my husband built for us. Life was great.

Not working outside of my home, I stayed busy raising our daughter and son and doing volunteer work. I became active in the PTA, cofounded a theatre group for children, and eventually started a catering and event planning business. I was always active and busy, and I thrived on it.

This charmed life of mine came crashing down when I became sick fifteen years ago. My entire body ached and hurt with flu-like symptoms, and I was exhausted beyond belief. For several weeks I had a "hit by a truck" feeling. Initially, because it is so prevalent in my area, the diagnosis from my primary care physician was Lyme disease, even though the test results came back negative. I was treated with antibiotics, yet I got no relief. After more blood work, it was finally determined that I had been sick with parvovirus, and this virus set off an autoimmune response in my body.

Over the next year, I went to many doctors trying to figure out what was wrong with me. Eventually I was diagnosed with lupus, an autoimmune disease that can cause a lot of pain in the nerves, joints, and muscles. There is no cure, and the only treatment is medication to help with the pain and hopefully prevent the disease from progressing into vital organs.

Over the next eight years, I was able to manage the illness and continue going about my daily life. I would periodically go through "flares" that would often last for months. During these flares, the pain would be more intense and longer-lasting than usual and would make it difficult for me to sleep or participate in my daily activities. Yet I was always able to get through the flares and then get on with my life when they ended.

All that changed one day when I was challenged by an extremely stressful situation in a volunteer job. I didn't know how to manage stress well, and stress can trigger a lupus flare. And bring one on it did.

My life as I knew it changed dramatically after that time. The pain in my nerves, muscles, and joints was excruciating and I could not sleep, eat, shower, or do much of anything. My days were spent either in bed or on the couch watching TV. Because I was up and down due to sleepless nights, I moved out of the bedroom I shared with my husband and into the guest room on the main floor. I didn't want to disturb him, and the stairs were becoming too difficult for me to climb. I was confident that although this was the worst flare that I had ever had, it would end in a few weeks or months, just like all the others. Yet my confidence started to diminish as these days turned into weeks, weeks turned into months, and months turned into four long years.

My husband was my guardian angel during these years, taking care of the kids and managing the household after his long days at the office. I had once been an outgoing social person, but during this four-year period, I had become alienated from my friends and family. I was extremely underweight and severely depressed. I missed all the kids' school functions and had to cancel every attempt to spend time with friends. The pain medication was not giving me any relief, so I turned to alcohol to help numb the pain. I was barely existing and was simply a mess, inside and out. I had given up all hope. My once positive attitude was now one of misery and despair.

During these dark days, I became absolutely obsessed with my pain and illness. I was convinced that I could control the illness if I could just find the right doctor, the right combination of medications, the right diet, and so on. I read about lupus incessantly on the Internet, trying to find that "miracle cure" that my doctors did not know about. I went from one doctor to another, convinced that the next one would hold the cure I was seeking. I spent an excessive amount of money going to the best traditional doctors and alternative spiritual healers. I tried every diet that claimed to be a cure. None of this worked, and my poor family was suffering right along with me.

I finally became sick and tired of being sick and tired. What I was doing was not working, and my family was miserable watching me go downhill and drift farther and farther away. My sister did some research and found a month-long program in another state that helped people learn how to live with chronic pain and illness. After being accepted into the program, I was willing to give it a shot. I had nothing to lose at that point because I had absolutely no quality of life left.

During my month at the facility, I learned different techniques to help me deal with my pain. I started on a light exercise program, was taught how to meditate, and was introduced to helpful tools in the classes I attended. I gave it everything I could; I wanted my life back.

The most life-changing part of my stay there was being introduced to CPA. The people at the meeting really understood me. Although the source of our pain was different, the way it affected us emotionally was similar. The most amazing part was that the people in the fellowship that had some recovery in the program seemed serene and happy. They were able to laugh! I hadn't been able to even smile in a very long time, and I wanted the serenity that they had.

I soaked up everything I learned from the CPA meetings during that month. It was a surprise to me that I could go into the meeting in tremendous pain, but by the end of the meeting, I felt emotionally, and even physically, better. I experienced firsthand the ways the program works and improves lives. I was beginning to have hope again. When I returned home, I found that there were no CPA meetings in my state, so I started one at a local hospital. The meeting was well attended right away, and it continues to grow with new members finding us. We meet once a week and have regular members who come to every meeting. I get such joy when someone new comes into the meeting! Seeing others benefit from the program the way I have is heartwarming. The program works as we share with others who understand.

Chronic pain does not discriminate; in our meeting, we have men and women, young and old, and a diversity of racial, ethnic, and socioeconomic statuses. Within this fellowship, we are all able to guide and support each other to live a fulfilling and serene life, despite having chronic pain and illness. We do this by embracing the CPA principles through the literature and by working the Steps.

I learned that I had to go through the stages of grief—grief for the healthy body and abilities that I had lost due to my pain and illness. Now I believe my pain is actually a beautiful gift. In a way, I am fortunate to have lived through such pain and suffering, because now I can recognize the beauty in the simple things in life and understand what is really important. I have learned to have empathy for others and not to focus all my time and energy on myself. I have learned patience and kindness, and eventually, I learned how to laugh again. Getting my smile back has been one of the most appreciated gifts that CPA has given to my family and me.

Now I'm living a life that I never could have dreamed possible. Not just despite my chronic pain and illness but *because* of it. By working the Steps of CPA, I no longer have to worry about what the future holds or regret what has happened in the past. Today is the only day that matters. Everything else is in the hands of my Higher Power, and by taking life one day at a time, I am better able to handle whatever comes my way.

Today I am able to participate in life again, and my family and I could not be more grateful. I am once again a mom to my kids and a wife to my husband. I was able to send my daughter off to college this past year and know she didn't have to worry if I was OK. My son will be a senior in high school and is happy that I am "back." They see me keeping up with my exercise, meditation, CPA meetings, and socializing. Today I spent the afternoon gardening, something I never thought I would do again! My kids and husband tell me they are proud of me—the greatest compliment I could ever get. I hope I am showing them that out of my struggle came strength. And if that can help them in their own lives, that is another significant gift of my journey.

I have no control over my pain and illness, but it no longer controls my life either. Today I work to find balance in my life and to take everything easy and listen to my body, not fight it. Once I was able to fully accept my illness and realize that I had no control over it, I was able to turn it over to my Higher Power. All this I can now do as a result of working the Steps of CPA. I no longer say that I'm *suffering* with chronic pain and illness. I am living peacefully with it. *Suffering* is a state of mind.

So, no, chronic pain and illness were not in my plans, but this plot twist has shaped who I am today. My heart is full of gratitude and thanks to CPA. I like the person I am today, and that's a great place to be.

Letting Go of Fear and Resentment

I had to have a medical procedure, and my older daughter was supposed to pick me up afterwards because they wouldn't allow patients to take the bus or a taxi home. She forgot all about it and wasn't reachable. Fortunately, Dial-A-Bus was willing and able to get me home.

I was pretty hurt, but I've been working on the Fourth and Seventh Steps a lot and have been saying prayers for these Steps every morning. After I got home, I had the thought, "What was your part in this?" I needed to think more about what happened.

I live a fear-filled life and am working on letting go of the fear. One of the things I'm afraid of is whether or not I can count on my daughters if I become unable to take care of myself. I was testing my older daughter by not calling the day before the procedure to remind her about picking me up. I set us both up, and it was unfair.

When she came over in the evening to apologize, I told her that I could have called and reminded her and was negligent in not doing so. I said that I had let the incident go. In the past, I would have nursed the hurt for a long time, gotten into anger and resentment big time, and finally let it fade. Today, I was a different person and was able to invite a new outcome, one that brought serenity into my life and the lives of my loved ones.

Learning New Ways to Live with Pain through the Steps

I was a single mother of a wonderful eight-year-old daughter. I had a good job, a house and a car. I was almost thirty years old, and I was happy and living a good life. My main goal was to raise my daughter and provide a good education for her. I thought everything was going to be wonderful . . . until one day when I fell at work.

I didn't think much of the fall at the time, but I did report it to my supervisor. I finished out the day since I had only one hour left of my twelve-hour shift. I didn't know at the time how the fall would change my life in many ways.

When I arrived home and removed my shoes, I discovered a goose egg on the back of my left ankle, so I went to the hospital. The doctor there told me I had a ruptured Achilles tendon and to stay off my foot and see a surgeon in a week. He put a cast on my left foot and ankle and gave me crutches.

I gave my employer a note from the emergency room doctor and told him what the doctor said about not putting weight on my foot. My employer responded by telling me I needed to see the workers' compensation doctor, so I went within a week of the fall. My foot and ankle were hurting severely, but the new doctor took the cast off and told me I could return to my regular duties at work. I followed his orders.

My foot and ankle weren't getting any better, so I went back to the company doctor. He began doing injections in my foot and ankle, and he told me I needed to start physical therapy. I began therapy while continuing to work the same hours. My foot still wasn't getting any better; in fact, it was getting worse. A month or so after the fall, I went back again to the company doctor. This time, I took my records and x-rays from the emergency room, and the doctor recast my leg. I had to go back several times because I kept breaking the cast at work. Eventually the doctor gave me a walking boot.

A year-and-a-half went by, and I was still doing physical therapy and working as much as I could. The company doctor sent me to a specialist who performed various tests and told me I had reflex sympathetic dystrophy syndrome (RSDS). This was the first time I had ever heard of the disorder. The specialist performed surgery on my foot and ankle. By then, I had been in a cast and walking boot for about two years, was still on crutches, and the pain was still getting worse.

After more tests, I was referred to yet another doctor. Then both doctors said I had RSDS on my left side. The pain made walking difficult. It was a sharp, burning, cutting, stabbing, crushing pain. At times, the pain would get so bad that I didn't know if I could go on. As a result, I was sent to a pain doctor who treated me with a lumbar block, which is an injection in the spine. I had a negative reaction to the treatment, which resulted in a stay in the intensive care unit at the hospital. Although the block helped bring the pain level down, I couldn't have another one because of the reaction.

About three years after the fall, the doctor put me on light duty at work and told me to stay off my foot as much as I could. At first my employer was cooperative, but as time passed, I was required to stand on my feet more and more. At this point, the pain was out of control. People were starting to say it was all in my head, and I was starting to believe them. I wondered, "Am I going crazy or what?" I started seeing both a psychologist and psychiatrist, and they removed me from my workplace.

I was so miserable that I started withdrawing from life. I would cry at the drop of a hat, and I would yell at people for the smallest things. I was told that I was manic-depressive and was referred to an anger management doctor.

I was very scared. It was recommended that I try a spinal cord stimulator to treat the pain. I tried it, and it cut my pain level almost in half, which was good, because by now the original pain had spread and was in both legs and feet. Along with the stimulator, I had to take pain medications, attend physical therapy three times a week, and do exercises at home every day.

I also saw the anger management doctor, the psychiatrist, and the psychologist regularly. They were all telling me I needed to learn how to live with this and that I needed to learn a new way of thinking.

The pain made it difficult to sleep at night. I slept only two or three hours. I took so many different medicines that I had to write them down so I didn't forget which I had taken or how many I had taken. I found it difficult to think clearly, sometimes forgetting what I had just said or what I was doing.

Since the original injury, I have been through surgeries, different doctors, therapy groups, psychologists and psychiatrists, and an anger management doctor. There is still no hope for a cure in sight. Because of all the medications I have taken, my liver and kidneys have been damaged. My illness was very hard on my family and loved ones. Feeling like I had lost everything, there were times I didn't care whether I lived or died.

One day, not too long ago, I found CPA's website and started reading their Twelve Steps. It was as if someone had turned on a light for the first time after many years in the dark. I felt hopeful for the first time.

I sit here now, with a clear mind, knowing that I can live with the chronic pain. I follow the Steps each and every day because this program has given me back my life. Just a few weeks before finding these wonderful Steps, I had given up on any hopes and dreams. I prayed, "God, why don't you just take me . . . this is no life!" I was mad at the world. I was stuck in self-pity. It was always all about me. The Twelve Steps have shown me I can rise above my pain. I still live each and every day with chronic pain, but without the tools of the program and a Power greater than myself, I might have chosen to give up.

I have found that the Twelve-Step program works if you follow it, listen to others in the fellowship, and share your experience, strength, and hope. I have a wonderful CPA group I attend in my city. At each meeting, fellow sufferers come together to learn a new way to live with pain.

My family and friends want to know what has changed in my life. They say this is the first time they have seen me smile in years and that my anger is under control. I tell them that the fellowship of CPA has shown me the way back to my dreams, hopes, and smiles. For the first time in years, I'm going fishing and camping!

I know if I do the work of my Twelve Steps, I can handle what life hands me now. My Higher Power walks with me, a minute at a time and hour after hour, and that I can make it, just for today. I may still have a long road to go, but today, I have made it.

Moving beyond Denial

Is denial always negative? I don't think so. Sometimes I need to be in denial. I need time to adjust, to assimilate new information. I need to be protected from the avalanche of painful feelings and thoughts. It takes time to come to acceptance, particularly with unpleasant and unwelcome realities. So I think there are times in which denial is a gift.

The problem comes when the denial continues past the point where it is helpful and starts to become harmful. It is a problem when my denial keeps me stuck, unable to move forward, and prevents me from taking actions that will help me cope and remedy the problems at hand.

In Twelve-Step programs there is a saying: "Focus on the solution, not the problem." When I am in denial, I am not able to focus on solutions. I will stay in the problem unless I can *see* that it exists. Denial blocks my vision.

Honesty is vital. In this program, I have had to be honest about where the real problems exist. My tendency is to blame others and remain in denial about my own part. If I can't identify the problem, I can't change it. This is where Step Four is so helpful.

Sometimes it is not clear. I don't work and have recently faced my financial realities, which I have been in denial about for a long time. I keep trying to work. I keep seeking jobs, going to school, making plans, and taking on projects. All of which ultimately fall through, because I start when I am strong and have to let everything go when I get ill again.

The tricky part for me is, what am I denying? Am I in denial about my ability to work? Or am I in denial believing I can't work when I can, if I just find the right position? Whichever is true, I gotta' eat!

I want to blame my illness, my former spouse, and the government on the lack of sufficient funds. All may have played a part, but I have no control over any of that. So I work the first three Steps. I accept that my life is unmanageable, I trust my

Higher Power, and I turn my denial and all my concerns about money over to my Higher Power. I do my Step Four inventory and look at my part. In Step Five, I share it with my sponsor and ask her for some suggestions. I ask my Higher Power for help. In Steps Six and Seven, I own my shortcomings and surrender them to my Higher Power. In Steps Eight and Nine, I make amends. In this case, the amends are mostly to myself. Then I work the last three Steps, doing the next right thing, one minute after the next: I pray for guidance. Wash the dishes. Do the laundry. Pay today's bills.

Using the Twelve Steps is the only way I have found to get beyond my denial. Program principles remind me that today I can pay for groceries and that one day at a time, I am OK. More will be revealed in God's timing, not mine. It is my faith and belief that my Higher Power cares that give me the courage to let go of denial and begin to work on the solutions. If I stay in denial, I won't do what I can to address my financial problems, such as assessing my expenses and cutting back on some of them. The choices I make today create my tomorrow. So with the help of my Higher Power, I move beyond denial and begin to make a plan.

Acceptance Gave Me Peace . . . Makes Me Grin

This is how it seemed to me: I went to work one day and had some back pain. I had back pain before and wasn't too worried about it. The next day, it was a bit worse. I still went to work. The third day, I asked to work from home. It was too painful to sit. I had a doctor's appointment later that afternoon for an unrelated matter. I stood in the waiting room while everyone else sat comfortably. On day four, I could no longer sit or stand still, but I could walk and lay down. I went to my general practitioner, got a prescription, and was told to rest. I worked from home again that day. The fifth day, I rested—I had no choice. I could no longer walk, stand, or sit without excruciating pain. Each trip to the bathroom was a horror.

To me, life changed dramatically in five days. There was a firm line in my life. Before I crossed that line, I traveled by rail, storm chased, volunteered building trails in our national parks, went cave crawling, and cycled. I loved to walk. I did stand-up comedy, performed in improvisational theater, and wrote sketch comedy. I took care of the house and the cars. I carried heavy litter boxes upstairs, vacuumed the house, and loved to cook. I mowed the lawn and shoveled the snow. I saw all the Oscar-nominated films the year they were nominated. I drove Route 66. I shopped for groceries. I volunteered as an emergency responder.

But after I crossed the line, on that fifth day, I rested. At first, I was not concerned. The doctors would fix it. It would take time, but they would fix it. They had always fixed me before. I didn't realize how harmful that false belief would become as my journey progressed.

I could fill a lot of pages on how the doctors tried, and failed, to fix me. I couldn't let go of the thought that my body was fixable. I remember the doctors telling me it wasn't, more than once, but I could not believe it. The miracle of medicine could surely fix it. I just had to find the right solution, the right answer. (This makes me grin.)

In the interim, I wasn't able to go to work. I feared losing my job, financial insecurity, boredom, and lack of purpose. I feared what would happen to my mother, whom I prided myself on caring for. What would happen to the house? I looked for help. The more doctors I met and listened to, the more frightened and worked up I became. Until, I suppose it's reasonable to say, I just went loopy.

My body was broken, but I was also broken mentally and spiritually. I was angry and lashing out at people all around me. I thought folks were out to get me. I knew about the Steps. Steps had helped me put down the drink. "Fixed." Steps helped me lose weight. "Fixed." Steps helped me become a better worker. "Fixed." Steps restored my sanity. "Fixed." But how could the Steps "fix" my unfixable body? I searched the Internet. I knew someone, somewhere, must have applied Steps to a similar situation and "fixed" it. I would find them. They would help.

This is how I came to CPA—physically, mentally, and spiritually broken but still hopeful the Steps could "fix" me. (This also makes me grin.)

At my first meeting, I gave out my phone number. CPA folks called me. I was suffering, and they listened. Sometimes that's all they did, and it was comforting. Sometimes they offered suggestions. It kept me coming back.

I began to listen at meetings. There was a "fix" for me. I knew it. I just hadn't done it: the First Step. I had to admit I was powerless over pain and illness, that my life had become unmanageable.

It seemed simple enough. Yet every time something needed to be done for the home, or snow needed shoveling, or trees cut, I tried to do it, even though my body couldn't. I would try different ways of doing things. I would buy gadgets. I would force my body to do as much as it could. And then I would suffer while my body tried to recover. Not just physically but emotionally, too.

I got a sponsor and began working the Steps in CPA. I was able to realize that my body didn't break in five days. My body and my health had been failing for a long time. I had my first surgery when I was sixteen and eight more before the back failure that brought me to CPA. I had been in denial a long time.

Denial is a strong force. We're not bad for being in denial. It's all we have to rely on for a while. But there came a point for me where I couldn't "fix" my body and denial couldn't force it to work. I could no longer tolerate the pain physically or emotionally. Pushing, forcing, suffering, and beating myself up didn't work anymore.

These two understandings—admitting I was powerless and awakening to my denial—brought me to a truth I had known for a long time. The universal "fix" for all things is acceptance. There is a church sign I used to pass by every day on my way to work that read, "If God is your copilot, switch seats." I was in the wrong seat, and acceptance moved me to the right one.

What I know today is, *acceptance ain't always my strong point.* Each time my body becomes unable to do something it was able to do the day before, acceptance is the answer, but it isn't always my first answer. That's OK. It's not where I start the journey that matters, as long as it leads to acceptance.

It is true, in five days my life changed. But my life changes every day. Nothing stays the same. I can accept the changes or fight to keep things the same. Today, I have come to believe that if I'm fighting, I'm working too hard. Acceptance removes the struggle and gives me peace.

I thought if I accepted my pain and physical limitations, I would be miserable, poor, homeless, and have nothing to contribute. That has not happened. I have all I need. I am generally happy. Even on painful days, I often find moments to smile. I have enough resources to meet my needs and just a little more. I have a roof over my head.

I used to think I cared for my mom, but my condition has "rightsized" me. We take care of each other now. Our relationship is more symbiotic. My condition offers my mother purpose. It has enriched our relationship in ways I never imagined. Most importantly, I still have purpose. There is purpose in welcoming each new person into CPA. I have been blessed to be able to continue to work, with accommodation. I can still offer laughter to others.

Finally, my sponsor shared a tip to help me accept change in my life today. When I finish a sentence, I add "just for today." So I may say, "I am in so much pain, just for today," or "I'm so grateful to be able to move with less pain, just for today." Everything changes and passes. The need to struggle, to force, to fight, to fear all diminish or completely dissipate when I remember that what is, is just for today. (That definitely makes me grin.)

Surrender to Win

Today as I share my CPA story, I am in my fifties, twice divorced and living alone. My two grown children live a thousand miles away. I've been in Twelve-Step recovery for twenty-four years. My struggles with chronic pain and chronic illness began about ten years ago when I couldn't understand why I was so tired all the time. A friend suggested that because of my history of drug abuse, I get tested for Hepatitis C, and I tested positive. I tried the conventional chemotherapy treatment, but I could not tolerate the side effects. I try to manage the illness with vitamins and diet, but the chronic fatigue is still a problem.

My chronic back pain, which worsens with age, seems to be caused by a combination of degenerative disc disease, arthritis, and a structural slippage in my lower back. I have pain when I stand, walk, or sit in certain positions for more than a few minutes at a time. Over the years, the amount of time I am able to be on my feet or be comfortable sitting has grown shorter, and the pain has become greater. When I became unable to work, I applied for disability benefits, which I now receive.

My ability to do things that I once did was steadily declining, year after year. I became more and more isolated from friends and family. I moved from my home to a warmer state to help care for my mother. I tried as best as I could to attend my Twelve-Step meetings, but I did not feel comfortable talking about living with pain and fatigue. I began to withdraw from the very fellowships that had saved my life. Because of my pain and illness, I did not feel connected to the people in the meetings like I had in the past.

The time finally came when I had to consider taking prescription medications. This was an agonizing decision for me, having been clean and sober for many years in Alcoholics Anonymous (AA) and Narcotics Anonymous (NA). When I was first ill, I had rejected the notion of taking anything stronger than over-the-counter pain medications. I thought it would be in conflict with my Twelve-Step programs. Being drug free had been my identity and salvation for many years. I heard others in AA and NA meetings say that they believed that anyone with a history of substance abuse could never take prescription pain medication safely. However, I had an AA sponsor who told me that if I really needed it to function, then it was not a relapse.

I was still very scared. Although I had heard stories from people who had relapsed from abusing pain medications, I also read that this does not have to be the case. There are provisions and safeguards in both the AA and NA literature about the need for some of us with pain and illnesses to take life-saving medications. I had to choose between being able to function and taking care of myself and my responsibilities or being basically bedridden

After years of denial, disappointments, and watching my old life slip away, I was feeling quite suicidal. I had hit a new bottom. In the midst of the pain, anger, and depression, I said to myself in desperation, "There has to be a fellowship out there for people like me. There has to be a Chronic Pain Anonymous out there!" I searched on the Internet and, sure enough, I found it.

I read every page of the website and then phoned one of the people listed as a contact. I can't remember exactly was said, but I felt an immediate, strong connection. He was so much like me—he was living with chronic pain, had a Twelve-Step background, and was living in the same area where I grew up. Talking with him gave me a strong feeling of hope. I signed up for an online meeting, and I started reading the posts. I introduced myself online, and many people welcomed me. I learned about the telephone meetings and proceeded to call in for every meeting. I listened to what everyone had to share, got on the phone list, and started calling people. It was wonderful to make friends with people who had the same experiences as me. It was the first time in a long time that I felt like I did not have to hide anything. I started working the CPA program the same way as I had done with my original Twelve-Step fellowship—I began with purchasing the recommended books and reading them daily.

One day, after hearing someone share at a phone meeting, I had a revelation that made me a free man. I felt liberated once I understood that I couldn't move on with my life until I truly accepted where I was in that moment. The fear was that acceptance of my pain and illness would consume me, but I discovered just the opposite. I had to surrender to win, just like in my first Twelve-Step program.

Today I can state openly—I am a person living with chronic pain and illness. I don't want to be, but it is a fact of my life. I accept this reality with all its challenges and disappointments, as well as the blessings and rewards.

One day at a time, I take my medications responsibly, and it helps control my pain and my sobriety remains intact. All is not perfect, since some of the side effects are challenging to me, and I sometimes still feel guilty about taking these medications. It is a huge comfort to have confidantes in the CPA program with whom I can speak honestly about my feelings and my medications.

Over time, I started taking on service positions—with much reluctance, but others believed in me even when I didn't believe in myself. Soon, another miracle happened—I was able to help others again. What a wonderful feeling! It seemed like it had been so long since I had felt like I had anything to give to others. There is a program saying I had learned years before, "you have to give it away to keep it," which was easy to forget when I was so busy focusing on myself. I have learned that when I focus on the positive, the positive will grow, and if I focus on the negative, then the negative will grow.

The fellowship in CPA is an important part of my recovery. I know people all over the world with similar feelings and challenges and have a place where I can share and am understood. Well-meaning friends and family try, but they can't really understand the experience of living with chronic pain and illness. Since there are no face-to-face CPA meetings in my city yet, I rely on the telephone meetings.

Today, I have something to look forward to in life. The service work I engage in has given me purpose once again. Instead of judgment, we have inclusion. The CPA Twelve-Step fellowship of love and understanding came along just in time to save me from myself.

I Can Be Happy, Even in Pain

When I first came into CPA, I was a confused mess emotionally. The first sixty-one years of my life, I was in good health, exercised daily, and was health conscious. I tried to do the things I felt would keep me healthy. I thought I was doing everything right . . . except, it didn't work out the way I planned. Suddenly, at age sixty-one, I was driven to bed by excruciating pain.

I then went on a quest to find a solution, as probably most people do. I tried lots of remedies and read a lot about my condition and about pain. I gathered information, tried different treatments and medications, but it became apparent to me that my pain was not going to go away. Gradually, I came to accept that it was probably a permanent part of my life. Accepting this was very hard for me.

I have now been in pain for six years. I have adjusted, made changes in my home for more comfort, left my job as I could no longer sit for long, stopped driving due to pain, lost some friends, and made some new ones. I moved to a new city that was closer to family because I sensed my own increasing vulnerability and fragility. I was feeling afraid of the unknowns and what the future would bring.

But since I've been going to CPA meetings, reading the materials, and reaching out to my Higher Power, I have a new level of peace and contentment. I believe it comes from being part of a group, feeling less lonely, and getting comfortable with the fact that I am powerless over this pain. In a sense, I have admitted defeat, and the irony is that by doing that, I feel empowered.

I have tools to help me with whatever might come my way. I have a fellowship that I'm connected to, where others listen and understand. And I have trust in my Higher Power, which has never promised me that I won't suffer, but it has guaranteed me that I will never be alone. I love the slogan *Let Go and Let God.* I have had to do this. I have had no choice.

When I came in to CPA, I was not coping well on my own. I was lost and confused. Today, I feel much more centered knowing that I have a group that understands me. I have a lot more peace now, and it keeps increasing.

I accept my pain as one of the things "I cannot change." With the help of my Higher Power, I have serenity and accept things as they are, just for today. I learned in CPA that I can be happy, even with my pain.

Keeping the Focus on What I Can Do

Raised by parents who were health conscious, I started off in life very healthy. Being athletic, I participated in many sports and physical activities. I was never one to be caught sitting around. So when I started noticing that I was getting tired a lot, after I had stopped drinking and smoking, I was really surprised. It seemed backwards to me. I thought that once I stopped doing damage to my body, it would miraculously rebound and I would live happily ever after. Well, it didn't work like that for me.

Soon after I got sober, I went back to school to get my bachelor's degree and continued on to get a master's degree. At the same time, I was working and trying to keep up the responsibilities to my family, friends, and program. I didn't let the tiredness stop me or even slow me down. During this same period, I also got married, had children, watched my father die, and left a stressful job. This all happened in a short time.

I tried many traditional and nontraditional methods to get rid of the physical symptoms and found a few things that helped, but nothing that really got me back to my old self. I was slowly learning that there was no silver bullet to completely get rid of my symptoms and that almost every remedy or medication caused side effects that were worse than the symptoms.

I was out surfing one day and started noticing that my lips and then my feet started tingling and feeling itchy. Then my hands started itching and feeling puffy. I knew this wasn't good and paddled back to shore. By the time I reached the sand, I felt really weak and had to sit down a couple of times as I tried to get back to my car. When I got to my car, I laid down on the pavement, unable to even get my wet suit off.

My little girl noticed me and called my wife over; she became alarmed and called a lifeguard. The lifeguard asked me a few questions and then called the paramedics. By now, I was shaking uncontrollably and felt extremely cold inside. It felt like I was lying in a meat locker, not on a sunny beach.

The paramedics told me that I was going into anaphylactic shock and would be transported to a local hospital for treatment. I stayed in the hospital for ten hours and was eventually released, after they had given me medications to counteract the effect of whatever had gotten into my system.

After this attack, my symptoms increased from fatigue to feeling achy all over my body. My symptoms were difficult to deal with, but they would come and go. I'd feel sick and tired for a day or two, then feel better. Over time, the symptoms lasted longer and longer. It felt like I was catching a cold or the flu, over and over again. Then, gradually, I began to realize that you can't have a cold or flu for months at a time.

I went to traditional doctors, nontraditional doctors, homeopathic practitioners, acupuncturists, and chiropractors. I tried numerous alternative healing methods, some so alternative I would be embarrassed to recount them.

Luckily, my Twelve-Step training kicked in and guided me to start looking at what I *could* control. This helped me let go of the negative feelings of frustration and anger long enough to look for a Twelve-Step group that could help me.

I knew from my miraculous experience of being saved from my substance abuse addiction that there might be a way to have the same kind of help with this new challenge in my life. It even occurred to me that I might have to start the group myself.

After doing a little research online, I stumbled onto the CPA website and almost cried with relief. There it was! I didn't have to go through months of work to get a new fellowship going. It already was there, just waiting for me to show up!

Many years have gone by since then. I have stopped trying to figure out what exactly happened that day out in the ocean. I focus on what I can do, which turns out to be quite a lot. I show up at CPA phone meetings and do acts of service and work the Steps on a daily basis.

The Steps, for me, include daily reading (from CPA and spiritual literature), writing gratitude lists, journaling, prayer (in the morning and many times throughout the day), and meditation (usually in the morning). I work the Steps with the guidance of a sponsor and also attend a spiritual center near where I live.

This Twelve-Step spiritual practice has evolved over time. It has brought peace, joy, beauty, and a tremendous sense of value and purpose to my life.

I still work full time; drive approximately two hours per day, five days a week; and keep up with the demands of family, career, and friends. I also am able to study several hours per week for a licensing exam in my profession. I wouldn't be able to do any of this if it weren't for the loving, miraculous Higher Power working in my life.

Yes, my life still feels very challenging and difficult. I know I couldn't have handled this level of difficulty if I hadn't had the experience of spiritual recovery prior to my getting sick. And I still get overwhelmed, quite frequently, when I am feeling really sick and facing a rough week filled with far more things than I think I can handle. Usually I can catch myself, however, and focus on the next thing in front of me to do, instead of dwelling on how I am going to keep this up for the next ten years.

I have learned to break things down into really small pieces. I don't take my life one day at a time so much as one moment at a time. I take lots of breaks and practice lots of self-care. This includes hot baths, massages, music, naps, listening to comedy, getting outside, just gazing at the sky, reading good books and magazines, walking in the grass, spending time with people I care about, or watching a good movie.

I haven't been able to get rid of my illness. However, I have learned how to live with it and not let it ruin my life. I have learned many lessons from facing and dealing with my challenges. I've come to believe life is designed to help me evolve and grow spiritually.

When I look at life this way, I don't feel resentful about the challenges. I just practice using the tools that I have available from CPA to work through the difficulties and then pass on what I have learned to others.

It used to seem like a curse to have a chronic illness. Now I don't see it that way. I have definitely learned to be a more compassionate, patient, and caring person as a result of my illness. I am grateful for these valuable qualities.

I Look Forward to the Day Ahead

Everything was right in my world! I had reached eight years of continuous sobriety in the rooms of AA, and I was preparing to move to a new state. Romance had blossomed in my life with an old friend I'd known for years in my working world. Things could not have been better.

I do remember noticing that what I had considered my "normal aches and pains" had increased substantially. I blamed it on the arthritis that my mom and brother complained of; what else could it be? My main concern in this new relationship was that I seemed to have much more energy than my prospective partner. What if he couldn't keep up?

Fast-forward a couple of years, and those aches and pains had become daily chronic pain. When I finally began seeking medical help, I was very lucky to have a doctor who recognized what was going on and sent me to a rheumatologist. In short order, I had the diagnosis of fibromyalgia. No cause, no cure, and not much to be done about it. Although I was told it was not progressive, I became more and more discouraged as I found the pain and fatigue levels increasing rather dramatically.

By then, I had a strong foundation in the Twelve-Step process, and as a result of my years in AA, I had learned that just about anything in my life could be made easier by putting those Twelve Steps into action. So I began using the first three Steps, just replacing the word "alcohol" with "pain." I was powerless over my pain and believed in a Higher Power who could help me deal with it. I worked at turning my pain and fatigue over to this Higher Power on a daily basis.

I had found a couple of online support groups for people dealing with fibromyalgia, but most of the people involved seemed to live in the problem instead of focusing on the solution. I had learned that by using the Twelve Steps, I could turn my focus to living as comfortable and serene a life as possible, in spite of the pain and fatigue. I began searching the Internet for a group relating to pain, and much to my surprise, one day I found a website for CPA! It was "under construction," so I e-mailed the person whose name was listed and found myself in contact with one of our cofounders. He encouraged me to check back frequently, which I did, until the website was complete and the first online meeting of CPA began.

Over time, I became more and more involved in the group and began to lead online discussions regularly. As I "met" others living with chronic pain and illness, I saw that it didn't matter what my diagnosis was. This recovery program, which utilized the Twelve Steps and Traditions, made it possible to climb out of the dark hole of depression and self-pity and begin focusing on the good things in my life. The pain was still there. I still didn't have any energy, but my whole attitude had changed, and I awoke each morning looking forward to the day ahead. I continue to do so!

Oh, and that relationship I moved for? We've been married fifteen years now, and he has never wavered in his commitment to loving me "in sickness" as well as in health. I am blessed.

Healthy in Mind, Heart, and Spirit

My life was a fairy tale. I was thirty-six years old, exercised regularly, and was strong and healthy. I was married to the man of my dreams, and we lived in a beautiful house with our lovely young daughters. My husband was a successful physician, and I was active with community volunteer work, school activities, and a full social calendar. My career was moving forward with the recent completion of a two-year postgraduate program of study.

Little did I know my perfect world was about to disappear. After a week of high fever and coughing, I was diagnosed with pneumonia. It was promptly treated, and I seemingly returned to full health. However, over the months following my pneumonia, I developed a series of unexplained symptoms: urinary, neurological, cardiac, gastrointestinal, and increasing fatigue. Despite going from specialist to specialist, no illness was identified. Within a year, my health had deteriorated to the point that I was no longer able to get out of bed. It was finally determined that I had chronic fatigue syndrome. This was not a well-received diagnosis. The medical community did not believe the illness existed, nor did my spouse. However, after everything else was ruled out, it was concluded that it was the correct assessment of my condition.

My spouse and I sought answers around the country, although there were very few treatments for this poorly understood illness. In the meantime, my life had come to a standstill. The illness and loss of my role in the family took its toll on everyone. I was no longer able to care for my family, so someone was hired to take care of the children and the household chores, with my husband stepping in as much as he could. I experienced profound grief for the life I had known that was now erased. It saddened me deeply to be unable to participate in my children's lives. Friends stopped calling. My sense of identity was blurred. The map for my life was no longer valid. I felt lost and confused.

My symptoms waxed and waned as I rode the roller coaster of chronic illness. There were good weeks and bad weeks, with no way to prevent symptoms from showing up and no way to control them once they did. My expectations of myself shifted to adjust to my new life. Completing simple tasks was cause for celebration. When I was able to get out of bed, shower, and put on clothes all in the same day, it was a major achievement.

For a long time, I held on to the belief that I'd soon be back to normal. Life would finally look familiar again, and I would be able to return to being the person that I was before I became ill. I read that many people became well after five years, so I had reason to hope that I would be one of them. This was not how the story ended. Instead, during those five years, I lived through a series of relapses and remissions. I'd be strong and feel like my life was back on track, only to lose it all again with the next bout of fatigue, pain, sleep disturbance, and cognitive impairment. I became despondent over my situation. It was beginning to appear that I would never be my old self again. After the five-year mark came and went, I sunk into a depression. I finally had to come to terms with the fact that my life was irrevocably changed and that I would have to let go of the dreams I had for my future.

I went through despair, self-pity, and thoughts of suicide. Life had lost its meaning and purpose. When I thought it couldn't get worse, my husband left me. As a result of my illness and my spouse's drinking, my marriage fell apart.

As often happens, the worst possible event transforms our life and becomes a gift in disguise. Working the Al-Anon Twelve-Step program I saw many aspects of my life change and improve, not just ones related to alcoholism. This led me to wonder if the Steps, principles, and tools of the program would work for living with chronic illness and pain. A few of us with Twelve-Step experience and an active physical disease got together in a private home to explore the possibilities. We earnestly began working the program with an in-depth study and application of the Steps.

We began our CPA meetings with the Serenity Prayer. Just by turning a kaleidoscope a teeny bit, the picture changes dramatically. When I stopped trying to focus on what could not be changed and started to work on what I could change, I discovered my attitude was what needed changing the most. I learned that how I perceive my life is what brings me happiness, not whether I can do things the way I used to do them. I found joy and laughter again.

My illness cannot be cured and treatments are experimental, yet for years I relentlessly searched for answers. Many of us with a poorly understood illness or pain optimistically keep seeking, looking under every rock, often finding many a charlatan or dead end. Insanity lies in doing the same thing over and over, expecting different results. Being able to surrender my illness and myself to my Higher Power helped me to live my life rather than see it as a problem to be fixed. I came to understand that although I am powerless over my illness, I am not helpless. I have choices. I can choose to eat well, get enough rest, and be with people who understand my illness and accept me as I am. I can choose to focus on what works in my life rather than on what doesn't work.

There is a lot of shame that goes along with any illness. In working the Steps, I did an inventory that included who I am in my new circumstances. Through the fellowship, I have learned how to accept myself just as I am and to know that I am a person of worth. I don't have to earn a living to be of value. I no longer compare myself to others or to what I used to be. Through service work, I have come to recognize how much I have to share with others.

In working the Steps with my sponsor, I chose to make amends to my family. I realized how often I expected my family to be sensitive to my needs, but I was not willing to be just as sensitive to their needs. After all, I was the sick one; didn't I deserve special treatment? When I don't feel well, my character defects are often at their peak. With CPA, I no longer had to be the melodramatic, poor, suffering victim. I could take responsibility for my actions and words. Just because I was in pain did not mean that I had to make others suffer along with me.

With CPA tools, the quality of my life improved, even though the illness itself was still active. When I awoke in pain and with little energy, I used to believe the entire day was a loss. In the program, I learned that I could start my day over again at any time, which opened up new possibilities. I soon discovered that my strength often improved in the afternoons, so waking up ill was not a predictor of how the rest of the day would unfold.

The familiar slogans of Twelve-Step groups were readily applied to my life with illness:

One Day at a Time. With an illness that was unpredictable, living in the moment was liberating. I learned that I didn't have to project the worst possible scenario into the future. I could see the blessings, which I found each day.

Let Go and Let God. When I came to understand that I was not in control of my illness, I discovered serenity. On bad days, my simple prayer of "help me and thank you" gave me strength to get through another hour.

Attitude of Gratitude. Instead of focusing on all that I did not have, I learned how to shine the light on what I did have in my life. I would go through the alphabet, finding one thing for each letter that I was grateful for. At the end, I'd see how rich and wonderful my life was in that moment.

CPA is a fellowship of friends who understand the journey of recovery of one's spirit while living in a body that doesn't always do what we want. In this program of spiritual recovery, I discovered that we can choose to be healthy in our minds, hearts, and spirits. We say that recovery is the ability to live peacefully, joyfully, and comfortably with ourselves and others. With the help of the CPA Twelve-Step program, I am learning how to do that, one day at a time.

APPENDIX A

Step Four: Suggested Formats

There are many different ways to do our Step Four inventory. We are providing a few suggestions to get you started. This inventory is an honest evaluation of ourselves. Each person finds his or her own way to go about this process.

What follows are some ideas, but you are by no means limited to these suggestions. We use whatever tool assists us in this fact-finding process. We start out asking our Higher Power for guidance and talk it through with our sponsor and program friends. Our sponsor may have a specific method he or she would like us to use, or not. We have faith that the way will become clear.

Organize this process in whatever way works. It may be writing an essay, making lists, or designing a chart. The objective is to end up with an accurate and complete description of yourself that you can understand easily when you read it. We include our actions, our feelings, our emotional landscape, our thinking patterns, our motivations. If it seems overwhelming, set aside five minutes each day to add something to your inventory. It doesn't have to be perfect, but it does have to be started. As we do our inventory, the ways in which our serenity is blocked begin to emerge and we can then begin our path to liberation from the effects of our pain and illness. Although today this may be our first inventory, it won't be our last. We have found that more is revealed over time.

1. *Explore the Fourth Step inventory guides* used by other Twelve-Step fellowships, such as Al-Anon or Alcoholics Anonymous, as well as other Twelve-Step based publications that are available. There are many that are useful and can be adapted for use in CPA.

186 RECIPE FOR RECOVERY

2. *Use the Four Cs.* Try using the following questions to guide your inventory:
   - Did I *cause* the problem or incident?
   - How have I tried to *control* it?
   - Is it in my power to *cure* it?
   - Did my actions *contribute* to the problem?

3. *Search online* for lists of character defects and character assets, values, and morals. These can provide an excellent starting place.

4. *Use the column approach.* There are several suggested methods for organizing the Fourth Step inventory using columns. Some possible column headings include resentments, relationships, self-obsession and self-centeredness, shame and guilt, feeling victimized, fears, and assets. The book *Alcoholics Anonymous* (often referred to as the "Big Book") suggests the following columns: resentment, the cause, what part of myself was affected, my part (i.e., where was I to blame?), whom did I hurt, and what should I have done instead? A variety of examples can be found through an Internet search. There are also different worksheets available that you may find helpful in organizing your thoughts.

5. *Write your life story.* Some people simply write out their life's story in five-year increments. Putting our personal history on paper can provide the clarity we need to uncover all our character traits.

The Twelve Steps of CPA

1. We admitted we were powerless over pain and illness—that our lives had become unmanageable.

2. Came to believe that a Power greater than ourselves could restore us to sanity.

3. Made a decision to turn our will and our lives over to the care of God *as we understood Him.*

4. Made a searching and fearless moral inventory of ourselves.

5. Admitted to God, to ourselves, and to another human being the exact nature of our wrongs.

6. Were entirely ready to have God remove all these defects of character.

7. Humbly asked Him to remove our shortcomings.

8. Made a list of all persons we had harmed, and became willing to make amends to them all.

9. Made direct amends to such people wherever possible, except when to do so would injure them or others.

10. Continued to take personal inventory and when we were wrong promptly admitted it.

11. Sought through prayer and meditation to improve our conscious contact with God *as we understood Him,* praying only for knowledge of His will for us and the power to carry that out.

12. Having had a spiritual awakening as the result of these steps, we tried to carry this message to others with chronic pain and chronic illness, and to practice these principles in all our affairs.

Printed by permission of Alcoholics Anonymous.

APPENDIX C

The Twelve Traditions of CPA

1. Our common welfare should come first; personal recovery depends upon CPA Unity.

2. For our group purpose there is but one ultimate authority—a loving God as He may express Himself in our group conscience. Our leaders are but trusted servants; they do not govern.

3. The only requirement for CPA membership is a desire to recover from the emotional and spiritual debilitation of chronic pain or chronic illness

4. Each group should be autonomous except in matters affecting other groups or CPA as a whole.

5. Each group has but one primary purpose—to carry its message to people living with chronic pain and chronic illness.

6. A CPA group ought never endorse, finance, or lend the CPA name to any outside enterprise, lest problems of money, property, and prestige divert us from our primary purpose.

7. Every CPA group ought to be fully self-supporting, declining outside contributions.

8. Chronic Pain Anonymous should remain forever nonprofessional, but our service centers may employ special workers.

9. CPA, as such, ought never be organized; but we may create service boards or committees directly responsible to those they serve.

10. Chronic Pain Anonymous has no opinion on outside issues; hence the CPA name ought never be drawn into public controversy.

11. Our public relations policy is based on attraction rather than promotion; we need always maintain personal anonymity at the level of press, radio, television, film, and the Internet.

12. Anonymity is the spiritual foundation of all our traditions, ever reminding us to place principles before personalities.

Printed by permission of Alcoholics Anonymous.

Twelve Concepts of Service

1. The final responsibility and the ultimate authority for the CPA World Services should always reside in the collective conscience of our whole Fellowship.

2. The CPA groups delegate complete administrative and operational authority to their World Service Conference and its service arms.

3. As a traditional means of creating and maintaining a clearly defined working relationship among the groups, the World Service Conference, the Service Board of Trustees and its service corporation, staffs, and committees, and of thus ensuring their effective leadership, it is hereby suggested we endow each of these elements of World Service with a traditional "Right of Decision."

4. The "Right of Participation" ensures equality of opportunity for all in the decision-making process. Participation is the key to harmony.

5. Throughout our structure, a traditional "Right of Appeal" ought to prevail, so that minority opinion will be heard and personal grievances will receive careful consideration.

6. The World Service Conference recognizes the chief initiative and active responsibility in most world service matters can be exercised by the trustee members of the Conference acting as the Trustee Board.

7. The Trustees have legal rights while the rights of the Conference are traditional.

8. The Trustees are the principal planners and administrators of overall policy and finance. The Service Board of Trustees delegates full authority for routine management to its executive committees.

9. Good personal leadership at all service levels is a necessity. In the field of world service, the Service Board of Trustees assumes the primary leadership.

10. Every service responsibility should be matched by an equal service authority, with the scope of such authority well defined.

11. The General Service Virtual Office is composed of the Executive Director, selected committees, and staff members.

12. The Conference shall observe the spirit of CPA tradition, taking care that it never becomes the seat of perilous wealth or power; that sufficient operating funds and reserves be its prudent financial principle; that it place none of its members in a position of unqualified authority over others; that it reach all important decisions by discussion, vote, and whenever possible, substantial unanimity; that its actions never be personally punitive nor an incitement to public controversy; that it never perform authoritative acts of government; that, like the Fellowship it serves, it will always remain democratic in thought and action.

General Warranties of the Conferences

- Warranty One: "that it never becomes the seat of perilous wealth or power"

- Warranty Two: "that sufficient operating funds and reserves be its prudent financial principle"

- Warranty Three: "that it place none of its members in a position of unqualified authority over others"

- Warranty Four: "that it reach all important decisions by discussion, vote, and whenever possible, substantial unanimity"

- Warranty Five: "that its actions never be personally punitive nor an incitement to public controversy"

- Warranty Six: "that it never perform authoritative acts of government; that, like the Fellowship it serves, it will always remain democratic in thought and action"

One Day at a Time

One Day At A Time – I will make an effort to participate in the world. I will reach out and connect with another person. I can pick up the phone and call a friend, greet someone on the street, or I can smile at the clerk in the store.

One Day At A Time – I will put my focus on promoting the well-being of someone besides myself. I will take the attention off of me and my issues, and place it on the needs of another being.

One Day At A Time – I will pace myself and trust my body to guide me. I will not push when my body tells me it's time to stop. I will do half of what I think I can accomplish.

One Day At A Time – I will eat well and exercise in moderation. I will take an interest in my appearance and tend to my personal hygiene. I may dress comfortably, but I will try to look my very best.

One Day At A Time – I will ask for help when I need it. I will accept assistance graciously and be thankful. I will appreciate the people in my life who support me.

One Day At A Time – I will live each day to the best of my ability and take responsibility for my own happiness. I will notice the good in life and not dwell on the negative. I will count my blessings and enjoy all that I've been given.

One Day At A Time – I will remember that I am more than my pain or my illness. I will believe that I am perfect exactly as I am. I will accept whatever comes my way with an attitude of gratitude.

One Day At A Time – I will make an extra effort to be patient and gentle with myself and others when I am feeling irritable and frustrated. No blame, no shame. Just because I am in pain doesn't mean I have to be a pain.

One Day At A Time – I will create some quiet moments for myself. I can use them for inner reflection, reviewing my day, or strengthening my spiritual connections. Taking this time each day is a rich and rewarding gift to myself.

One Day At A Time – I will enjoy something that is fun. I will engage my mind in creative activities. I will try something different and be open to new possibilities.

One Day At A Time – I accept the conditions of my life as they are this day. Within any condition I can contribute to myself, my family, and my community. I am a valuable member of society.

One Day At A Time – I will acknowledge feelings of fear and anxiety as they rise up. When they appear, I will remember to put my trust in a Power greater than myself. I will have hope in knowing that this, too, shall pass, and I will have faith that I can thrive through anything when I do it one moment at a time.

APPENDIX F

The CPA Declaration

INTRODUCTION TO THE CPA DECLARATION

Some of us believe our problems are insurmountable. We have lived with pain and suffering for so long; we have given up hope for happiness. We believe any promises for positive change are only true for others, not for us.

The CPA program of recovery offers new attitudes and ways of thinking. We may start this journey with doubt, yet little by little, through our consistent efforts, we will discover a different way of life in which beneficial habits will begin to replace ones that once brought us misery.

Our spiritual recovery will be accomplished by being open to the experience, strength and hope shared by our friends in the fellowship. We will come to understand if we do what others have done, we will get what others have gotten. As we steadily work the Twelve Steps of CPA and engage in service, our relationship with chronic pain and chronic illness will no longer be adversarial. We will begin our day with gratitude and hope. Possibilities we never dreamed of will be part of our daily existence and we will begin to see that we can have a quality of life despite living with pain and illness.

So, with the little bit of faith and guidance that brought us to CPA, we begin. *If we are rigorous in our endeavor, we will be astounded by the results.*

CPA DECLARATION

1. *Fellowship, rather than loneliness and isolation, will be present in our life.*

2. *We will enjoy connecting with other people.*

3. *We will be compassionate and kind to ourselves as well as consider the needs of others.*

4. *Fear will be replaced by courage, strength and faith to rise and meet any challenges. We will even see challenges as opportunities for spiritual growth.*

5. *We will forgive those whom we perceive have harmed us so we can be free from the chains of the past.*

6. *Remembering progress, not perfection, we will approach each day with a positive attitude. We will choose to focus on gratitude, placing our attention on all that is good.*

7. *Our pain and illness will no longer be the primary focus of our day. We will feel serenity and peace regardless of what condition our body is in. Our body will not determine the joy we experience in life.*

8. *We will laugh and see the lighter side of situations.*

9. *We will value ourselves and believe we have something to give to the world. Self-pity will be replaced by a belief our life has meaning and purpose.*

10. *We will be open to new beginnings and no longer cling to how things were in the past.*

11. *We will believe we deserve to love and to be loved.*

12. *We will have faith in a Higher Power which does for us what we cannot do for ourselves. This Power is the foundation that will support and guide us as we move through each moment. Our life will be far better than we ever imagined possible.*

Literature Available from CPA

CPA literature can be purchased or downloaded at *http://www.chronicpainanonymous.org.*

The website lists all CPA meetings for anyone seeking to attend a CPA group. You can also learn how to start a CPA meeting in your community.

To contact CPA, write to: Chronic Pain Anonymous Service Board, 8924 East Pinnacle Peak Road, Suite G5-628, Scottsdale, AZ 85255, or visit the website at *http://www.chronicpainanonymous.org.*

Notes

Notes

Notes

Printed in Great Britain
by Amazon